MORE THAN WORDS

MORE THAN WORDS

· An introduction to communication ·

RICHARD DIMBLEBY
and GRAEME BURTON

METHUEN · London and New York

First published in 1985 by
Methuen & Co. Ltd
11 New Fetter Lane,
London EC4P 4EE

Published in the USA by
Methuen & Co.
in association with Methuen, Inc.
29 West 35th Street,
New York NY 10001

Typeset by
Scarborough Typesetting Services
and printed by
Richard Clay (The Chaucer Press),
Bungay, Suffolk

*British Library Cataloguing in
Publication Data*

Dimbleby, Richard
More than words: an introduction
to communication
1. Communication.
I. Title   II. Burton, Graeme
001.51   P90

ISBN 0–416–38060–3
ISBN 0–416–38070–0 Pbk

*Library of Congress Cataloging in
Publication Data*

Dimbleby, Richard
More than words: an introduction
to communication.
Bibliography: p.
Includes index.
1. Communication.
I. Burton, Graeme.
II. Title.
P90.D53   1985   001.51   85–7148

ISBN 0–416–38060–3
ISBN 0–416–38070–0 (pbk.)

For our families

CONTENTS

ILLUSTRATIONS AND FIGURES

ILLUSTRATIONS

FIGURES

ACKNOWLEDGEMENTS

We wish to thank Jackie Adams for patiently typing our rough drafts; Terry Williams for the cartoon; Kathy Lucas and Steve Thomas for many of the photographs, and all those who were willing to appear in the photographs; Patrick Woodrow for the storyboard; Heather Buttery who offered helpful and encouraging suggestions on our original outlines; Ernie Parsons and Neil McKeown who made useful comments on our typescript; past and present colleagues who have contributed to our ideas, especially Bryn Davies, Margaret Harvey, Chris Renwick, Robin Scott Beveridge, Philip Johnson and Steven Cowan; past and present students from whom we have also learnt; Gill, Nicholas and Caroline, and Maggie, Tom and Lottie, who have put up with our non-communication; and Jane Armstrong, our editor at Methuen, for giving us the opportunity to write and for helping us produce the book and complete the project.

We and the publishers would like to thank the following for their permission to reproduce material (every effort has been made to trace the copyright holders; where this has not been possible we apologize to those concerned): the Engineering Industry Careers Service for figure 14; *L'Express* for the original version of figure 25; BBC news and the *Sun* for illustration A; Software Limited for illustration G.

Richard Dimbleby, Graeme Burton   *January 1985*

PREFACE

'Just as toothpaste and mouthwash are really not the key to social success, nobody can give you a communication pill which will automatically transform you into a communication star.' (Myers and Myers, *Dynamics of Human Communication*, 1980)

WHY STUDY COMMUNICATION?

If you're looking at this book we assume you're interested in knowing more about 'communication' and interested in learning how to communicate more effectively.

Whether we like it or not we spend every moment communicating. We depend on this activity in our personal, social and working lives. So it makes sense to find out *what* we're communicating, *how* we're communicating and *why* we're communicating.

We believe the study of communication is about:

knowing – what happens when people communicate with themselves and with each other.

understanding – how that knowledge can be used to explain and interpret the processes of communication in everyday life.

skills – using this knowledge and understanding to enable us to communicate more effectively.

WHAT IS COMMUNICATION STUDIES?

Many school and college courses now carry this label in some form. Increasingly people recognize that being an effective communicator is an asset.

In the past the art of effective communication (being able to express your ideas and opinions and understand other people's) was thought to be based on 'correct' uses of language.

However, communication studies goes beyond this to include 'appropriate' uses of both language and other forms of communication. These are studied to enable us to understand and deal with people.

The art of communicating is not a natural process or an ability we are born with. **We learn how to communicate**. Therefore we may study what we learn in order to use our knowledge more effectively.

All communication involves the creation and exchange of meanings. These meanings are represented through 'signs' and 'codes'. Communication studies is concerned with the business of making and understanding 'signs'.

People seem to have a need to read meaning into all human actions. Observing and understanding this process can lead us to be more aware of what we are doing when we are communicating.

WHAT THIS BOOK OFFERS

This book helps you to develop skills and techniques of communicating.

It describes theories about communication in order to understand why and how the processes of communication work.

The what, why and how of communicating are the themes of this book.

Our aim has been to produce a readable book. We have simplified and abbreviated a good deal. We have not attempted to include discussion of all possible theories about communication and we have included only a few language-based activities. Readers who wish to follow up the ideas of this book with more factual detail and background information will find suggestions for further work at the end of each chapter and in the resource lists at the end of the book.

HOW TO USE THIS BOOK

The *general reader* may like to go from first to last page. Alternatively, you may prefer to dip into sections that particularly interest you. You may wish to use it as a source of reference.

The *teacher of communication* may want to use it as a course book and as a source of ideas for discussion, presentations and practical activities.

The *student* will find sections that provide an account of key concepts and understandings of communication with examples and suggestions for your own practical work. On your own or in a group we hope you will gain ideas for analysing other people's communication and for creating your own communications.

The format of each chapter will follow a similar pattern:

- brief summary of the whole chapter,
- a personal story beginning each section,
- general concepts and ideas,
- particular examples, applications and cases,
- review of the main elements of the chapter,
- practical activities to develop analytical and creative skills, with suggestions for further reading.

We hope that readers will explore the meanings of our illustrations as they relate to the sections and topics which follow them. In particular, these pictures may say something about people's values and views of others in terms of gender, age, status and occupation. We hope that any apparent stereotypes serve a purpose which will be revealed in the text and through reflective viewing of the pictures as captured moments of communication.

WHY ANOTHER BOOK ABOUT COMMUNICATION?

There are many books about communication. Some are about personal communication skills, some about the mass media, some about use of language, some about business communication. We have brought all of these topics together in one book to provide a general introduction.

Many of the available books are rather difficult to read because they contain a good deal of jargon and are aimed at graduate-level readers. We have tried to explain some of the jargon to create a book that is accessible to people in the final years of school, to students at colleges and to any interested reader.

SUPPLEMENTARY MATERIALS

Further materials for reference and practical activities associated with the topics of this book will be available at intervals from the publisher.

Richard Dimbleby, Graeme Burton   *January 1985*

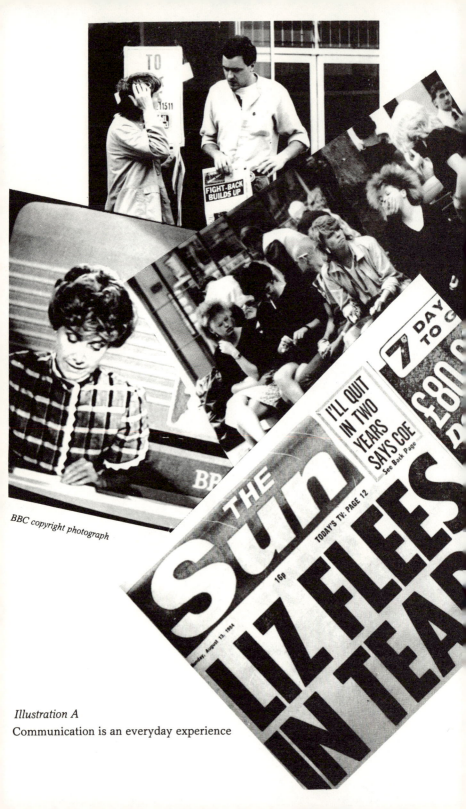

BBC copyright photograph

Illustration A

Communication is an everyday experience

·1· WHAT IS COMMUNICATION?

'One cannot not communicate.' (Watzlawick, Beavin and Jackson, *Pragmatics of Human Communication*, 1968)

This chapter provides a general introduction and background to the whole book by explaining four important aspects of communication:
1. How we experience communication, and how this experience can be analysed.
2. How communication serves our personal, social, work and play needs.
3. For what purposes we use communication.
4. Ways of describing and explaining communication processes.

---

1 HOW DO WE EXPERIENCE COMMUNICATION?

John's story

John was at his worst first thing in the morning. From the time that the alarm bell rang to the time that he took his ticket from the conductor on the bus into work, he was never more than half awake. And that half was the bad-tempered part. He would snarl at everyone in the house, including his father, who whistled good-naturedly from the moment he got up. It was the noise of the radio in the kitchen that forced John out of bed. That or his sister's record player. He would stumble downstairs, picking up the newspaper from the front door. The post had usually come by then. So if there was any, he would prop his letters up in front of him against the cornflakes packet, trying to decipher the writing through half-closed eyes. Otherwise, he just read the packet, moodily, looking for free offers and competitions. His mother usually spoke to him while she was frying eggs and bacon. But John was an expert at grunting in the right place, and didn't have much to say for himself. Finally he would look at his watch, collect his coat and bag on a run through the hall, and turn to wave goodbye as he tripped over the incoming cat, and down the path.

About John's story

If you were asked to spot the references to communication in this story, and in the previous photographs, probably you would refer to those objects which communicate. Things like newspapers and radios are what most people immediately associate with the word 'communication'. And even if we add items from the story such as the whistle or the wave of the hand, then still it might be said that we experience communication through such things. As we might say, they are means of communication.

1.1 Means of communication

In this case, communication is defined in terms of the means by which it takes place. It seems that if we are talking about radio, or painting, for example, then we must be talking about communication. But this isn't good enough because it doesn't tell us how the means of communication is being used. It doesn't tell us why the communication is happening. In fact, it doesn't tell us a lot of things, all of which partly answer our main question, what is communication?

Still we have to start somewhere, and it is useful to sort out how one describes the many means of communication that we use and experience. Not all of them are, strictly speaking, individual and separate forms. So we suggest that you use the following three terms:

(a) **Form of communication**
   is a way of communicating such as speaking or writing or drawing.
   Forms are distinct and separate from one another as far as they have their own system for putting the message across.

So, writing uses words, which are marks on paper made according to certain rules (grammar).

(b) Medium of communication
is a means of communicating which combines differ-
ent forms.

As a generalization, many of what we would call forms are ways of communicating which we control directly such as non-verbal communication (gestures, facial expressions, etc.).

But a medium often involves the use of technology that is beyond the control of most of us. So, for example, a book is a medium which uses forms of communication such as words, pictures and drawings.

(c) The media
are those examples of mass communication which
have come to be a distinct group of their own.

We are going to discuss these in chapter 5, and say something about what they have in common and how they communicate with us. Examples of these would be radio, television, cinema, newspapers and magazines.

These media are also distinctive in the way that they may include a number of forms of communication. For example, television offers words, pictures and music.

Again, the term 'media' often identifies those means of communication which are based on technology that makes a bridge between the communicator and the receiver. So, this book is one of those media, and communicates via the use of technology.

Comment

Some qualities of forms or media of communication are
'built in'. So, something like speech is necessarily transient. There is no permanent record of what is said. A magazine, on the other hand, has the quality of storing what it communicates, there is a permanent record on the page and we can go back to the communication any time we want to. Again, some means of communication involving technology seem to have a dominant quality of carrying messages. Examples of these would be satellites, or kinds of transport, which clearly help us communicate, but only in the sense of carrying our speech or our letters.

Some qualities of forms or media of communication are
imposed. For example, cartoons, whether in a newspaper or on

television would probably be described as funny, but they don't have to be. Serious cartoon films have been made. Commercial interests and film-makers have imposed a habit of using the medium in a particular way.

To take another example, we tend to think of radio as a broadcast medium. But this quality is also imposed, and is not a natural consequence of the technology of radio. The fact that CB radio has only recently been permitted in England is a consequence of decisions made by government. Setting aside problems of crowded airwaves, there is no technical reason why radio should not be used by us for exchange of messages, as much as for transmission.

All forms or media of communication extend the power of our senses. All the communication that we give or receive must pass through our five senses, especially those of sight and hearing. This is true even when we use some piece of technology to aid our communication. A public address system extends the range of the human voice. A tape recording extends our ability to communicate over distances, or even through time. It can be carried from place to place and can be kept for many years. Computers are interesting because they are also extending human powers such as that of memory. A computer never forgets what it has been 'told', and can do the same job over and over again.

There are other means of communication which don't easily fit into our usual descriptions of form, medium and the media.

These other signs are mostly seen in our everyday environment. Examples would be traffic signs, or special shop signs such as the barber's striped pole.

Look out for these other means of communication. Ask yourself why they exist, and what they communicate.

Most means of communication are intentional. That is to say, someone created them with the intention of communicating a message. This could include even unusual examples such as a church spire. It can be argued that this is intended to draw attention to the building, to its function and to a religion.

However, it is important to recognize that messages and meanings can also be understood in some cases where the means of communication is used unintentionally. For example, every day we deal with a flood of messages about our environment. Neighbours may not intend to tell us about their activity when they are using a lawnmower. But of course we do take a message about what they are doing and where they are from the sound of the lawnmower.

In chapter 2 we will see that this question of intention can be particularly important when understanding people's non-verbal messages. They may send these to us unintentionally.

1.2 Communication makes connections

In everyday experience we find that **communication is something which makes connections**.

The connections are made between one person and another, or between one group of people and another. Sometimes the connection is immediate, as when we talk face to face. Sometimes it is 'delayed', as when advertisers communicate with us through street posters. But still a connection is being made, mainly through what we have called forms or media. A 'form' is a means of making the connection. The act of communicating is the act of making this connection.

What flows through the connection are the ideas, beliefs, opinions and pieces of information that are the material and the content of communication. Our television set links us with the world at large through news programmes. Speech links us with each other.

But bear in mind the fact that being able to speak to someone doesn't mean that we can get across what we want to say. Having made the connection, we then have to learn how to use it to the best of our ability.

1.3 Communication is an activity

We experience communication as an activity.

It is something that we do, something that we make, and something that we work on when we receive it from others. In this sense, communication is not just about speech, but about speaking and listening, not just about photography, but about photographing and viewing photographs.

When we are talking to someone, we are actively engaged in making sense of what the other person is saying, as much as talking ourselves. For the same reason, it isn't true to say that watching television is passive. On the contrary, just as a group of people have been actively engaged in putting a programme together, so we are actively engaged in making sense of the programme – even if we are sitting down at the time.

1.4 Communication is learnt

Communicating is something that we learn to do.

In fact, we not only learn how to communicate, but we also use communication to learn how to communicate. This is what is happening in schools and colleges at the moment. It is what is happening as you read this book – we hope.

Our earliest experiences as babies include others talking and gesturing to us. We learn how to do the same thing, by practice and trial and error. There are some people who believe that we are born with some basic skills which help us learn how to talk and to understand what we see. Nevertheless, most of our communication skills must be learnt. An English baby, born in this country but brought up in Japan, will be Japanese, except in appearance. That is to say, that person will learn to communicate in the ways that a Japanese person does.

So, abilities such as talking or writing are not natural. They are taught us by parents, friends and school. And, as growing creatures, we want to learn at least some of these communication skills because we can see that they are useful. For example, to explain to others what we want.

The fact that we experience communication as something which we learn to do has important consequences for anyone studying the subject. It means that we should consider important questions such as why we learn, how we learn and what effect this has on us? Answers to these questions help explain other aspects of communication study, such as what effect television may have on us, or why we may have problems in communicating with others. So when we examine examples of communication in given situations, there is more to it than what is going on at the time. We must also examine what is behind the communication, what came before, what comes afterwards.

1.5 Categories of communication

We can divide our experiences of communicating into four categories.

These categories are loosely based on the numbers of people involved with the act of communication. They are a useful way of trying to define our field of study, like the terms 'form' and 'media'. Some forms or media belong more to one category than another, though there is no absolute rule. The remaining sections of this book are based on these categories.

(a) **Intrapersonal communication**
   is communication within and to the self.
   When we think, we are communicating within ourselves. We could be reflecting on the events of a day, or working out a problem in our heads. Arguments about how we think, for instance whether we use words or pictures when we think, have not been resolved.

   We also talk to ourselves, and write diaries for ourselves. Again, the person making and receiving the communication is us.

(b) **Interpersonal communication**
   is communication between people.
   Usually this category is taken to refer to two people interacting face to face. There are 'odd' examples which could fall within this category, such as a telephone conversation. And it is worth remembering that face-to-face communication takes place in situations where there are more than two people present. Examples of familiar interpersonal situations are an interview, a salesperson talking to a client and a conversation between friends in a café. It is the fact of face-to-face contact, and the emphasis on speech and non-verbal forms of communication which make such situations in this category distinctive.

(c) **Group communication**
   is communication within groups of people and by groups of people to others.
   In this case it is convenient to make two more divisions: small groups and large groups. Small groups behave differently from pairs. But they still interact face to face. More will be said about them in chapter 3. A family is a small group, so is a group of friends out for an evening together, or a committee meeting at work.

   Large groups behave differently from small groups, not only because they are bigger, but because they are often brought together or come together for purposes that are rather different from those of small groups. Examples may include an audience at a concert and some kind of business organization or company. It is this last example that we will concentrate on in chapter 4.

(d) **Mass communication**
   is communication received by or used by large numbers of people.
   In making a definition based on numbers, we don't have to

be specific. An open-air concert for a thousand people might reasonably be called mass communication. The point is that the numbers involved at any one time are much bigger than anything we would reasonably call a group. It is the fact of large numbers being involved that makes this category special, in terms of who is able to control the means of communication, and in terms of what its effect may be. This will be explored in chapter 5.

There are two kinds of examples to cite. The mass media form one subdivision, where obviously we are talking about large audiences. Apart from the examples already given, it is worth adding those such as the pop record/cassette industry.

The telephone and postal systems are examples of the other kind of mass communication. There may not be large audiences for the kinds of communication which are sent out. But such systems are used on a large scale, by thousands of people at any one time. So they do fit this category on general grounds of number.

Comment

In examples of real situations we may notice that communication occurs that fits within more than one of these categories. For example, the publicity manager of an organization might take notes (intrapersonal communication) before a meeting (group communication), after which he might place a display advertisement in a newspaper (mass communication).

One other point to notice is that study of one of these categories of communication contributes to an understanding of what is happening in another. For example, if we look at how a group of people interact in the typing pool of an insurance company, then how they behave as a group is also explained partly by how they behave in pairs, which is also explained partly by how they communicate within themselves.

To put it rather simply, how we talk with others depends on how we think and how we see ourselves, and how we talk in a group depends on how we talk with others.

2   WHY DO WE COMMUNICATE?

Sarah's story

It was Friday night and a bad time for Sarah. The mirror was no help, so she took it off her wall. The darkening evening outside her window was cheerless, so she drew the curtains. She tripped over her sports bag as she turned away from the window, so she kicked it.

What would be the third thing to go wrong, she wondered. Last week she had lost her Saturday job. Not enough customers coming to the wine bar, he had said. Business is bad. Not so bad, she had found out, that he couldn't keep on the other part-timer. And we all know why he kept her on, thought Sarah darkly to herself.

And now she had broken up with Neil. She had to admit that they hadn't been getting along so well. But she hadn't expected him to actually break it up. It wouldn't have been so bad if it had been her idea. . . . So here she was, looking at the wallpaper, bored as hell, and not feeling good about herself.

'Is there something wrong with me?' she wondered. 'I just couldn't stand him sulking every time I wanted to go off and do something different, maybe go out with some girl friends. Still, maybe I should have been more considerate. Maybe there's something about me that puts them off. After all, he's not the first to go.'

Sarah's morale sank again. She looked at the clothes that she had put out to wear before that abrupt phone call.

'I'd better do something before I commit suicide,' she thought.

It was then that she remembered that O'Rourke had given her a further day's pay in lieu of notice. Not that he had to, she thought, to be fair. But it meant that she could go shopping in town. Because she had some money, and because now she wouldn't be working tomorrow.

'I'll ring Julie,' she decided. 'Perhaps I can go round there and talk things over with her. That's what I need to do – talk to someone – get it all in proportion. And Julie might want to come to town tomorrow as well. New clothes and a day out . . . and who knows who we might meet,' thought Sarah.

About Sarah's story

This tells us something about what communication does for us. There has to be a reason why we decide to communicate in the first place. If we consider what Sarah did, and what she was going to do, then it is clear that her thinking was a piece of 'intra-personal communication', and that when she rang Julie she would be within the category of 'interpersonal communication'. And when Sarah talked over her situations and her feelings with herself, she was impelled to communicate by something within herself. The same could be said of her conversation with Julie – when it took place. Sarah wanted to feel better about herself, she wanted someone to talk to. We all want something to happen through communicating. In other words, we have needs, which communicating can help to satisfy.

2.1   Needs for communication

Survival

We communicate because we need to survive.

In wealthy northern countries it seems strange to talk about survival, especially in its basic senses of warmth, food and shelter. Yet some of our communicating is still about these physical needs. For example, we would communicate in order to rent a flat (shelter). The flat might be rather different from a village hut, but it still does the same job.

Co-operation

People need to communicate in order to co-operate.

And from this need – it could be argued – spring most of the others that we are about to outline. For example, the next but one point is about social needs. It would seem pretty obvious that our needs to form kinds of social groups actually comes from our needs to co-operate in order to survive. Organized groups in a tribal situation can hunt together, provide shelter and protection for the weak (including children). They would use communication to get along with others, and to work with them.

Personal

We communicate because we have personal needs to satisfy.

This reminds us that, just as survival was about more than physical things, so also our needs are not merely physical.

We have a personal need to feel secure within ourselves. And this leads to the other needs – to have a good opinion of ourselves, to feel we are wanted and valued.

In the story above, Sarah had begun to feel badly about herself, to feel there might be something wrong with her. She wanted to be wanted and valued, and so was going to turn to a friend for comfort. Communication with and from others helps satisfy these security needs. All this underlines the important fact that communicating isn't just about practical and physical things, like buying 6 pounds of potatoes. It is also about non-physical things such as emotions, feelings and ideas. So these personal needs are behind communicative acts such as dressing in the right way for an occasion; having 'a cry on somebody's shoulder'; giving people presents.

Social

We communicate because we have social needs, we need to be involved with others.

This follows naturally from the last two points. We need to have friends, because friends support each other, making one another feel good: thus it relates to personal needs. And we need to get along with our work-mates, because working with people is about more than job tasks: thus it relates to needs for co-operation.

When one talks about being involved with others, this could be in terms of number (pairs or groups); in terms of what binds those involved (friendship or love); and in terms of what description we may give the involvement (family or club). Here one can argue that needs may be of differing intensity and more or less permanent.

In social terms, communication helps us join with others, to know them and be known by them. We are bound together by ties of communication, which represent the feelings within us for each other. Even when deeper feelings are not involved, still communication is the binding force which holds groups together.

Practical

We need to communicate in order to hold our society together, in a practical sense.

The bigger the society, the more communication is needed. It is the practical problems of running large businesses, for example, that have led to the development of new forms and media of communication. Data processing with computers seeks to solve the problem of handling huge amounts of information quickly, using new means of electronic communication. These more practical social needs are to do with what goes on outside ourselves. They are to do with making the whole system work for us: hospitals, schools, manufacturing, government. Without communication, none of these pieces of society would function. They make our day-to-day existence possible.

Economic

Some of our practical and social needs are also economic needs.

That is to say, we may communicate as part of economic activity. Advertisers communicate in order to promote a product or service, and in order to maintain their own business activities. And, from another point of view, our communication at work comes from economic needs. We need to earn money. In this sense, personal economic needs become an extension of survival needs.

Information

We communicate because we need to give and receive information.

In this case, especially, the connection between need and purpose may be obvious. What we need to do relates to what we think we will achieve once we have done it. We may need to find out the time when a bus leaves town because we want to go somewhere. So also, when we telephone the bus station, our purpose in communicating is to find out the bus time. The need is behind the communication, and is what motivates us. The purpose is in the communication, and is what directs it.

Also, in a more general sense, **we need information in order to maintain a sense of what the world is like and how we relate to it**. So, on a large scale, we are avid viewers and readers of news, because this tells us about people, events and places in our whole country, as well as the rest of the world. On a smaller scale, we are great gossips and conversationalists, because we want to find out what is going on, and what people are up to, in the piece of the world that is our everyday lives.

Play

We communicate because we need to play with ideas and stories.

In some ways this is the most interesting kind of need. Because it isn't about physical well-being or about social relationships in any obvious sense. We wouldn't die, and our society would not end if we did not play in the various ways that we do. Yet it remains a fact that we have this need to play, as is shown by many of the things that we do in our everyday lives.

First, there is the kind of **play which we initiate**. Under this heading would come activities such as telling stories within a group of friends, writing poetry or literally playing games.

Second, there is the kind of **play which is initiated from sources outside us**, but which we are still actively involved with. Under this heading would come radio quiz games, television drama, computer games and the whole range of products offered by the entertainment industries. The strength of our need to play, in this second instance, can also be judged simply in terms of the huge amounts of money which we pour out each year on things like records, video recorders and the television licence fee.

It seems that humans have an innate urge to use their imagination and to be creative. Clearly, there is more to life than mere transactions. Our control of forms of communication, especially those using words and pictures, enables us to make up things that might happen, or create situations that will never happen. In particular, we love stories – fictions which give us amusement and pleasure. Through a story we can be in places which we may never visit or meet people whom we would fear to meet. We can be involved with a relationship which reminds us of one which we once had, or one which we would like to have.

3 WHAT DO WE USE COMMUNICATION FOR?

Tina's story

Tina White was a young reporter on the Midwestern Evening News, *a small provincial paper in the north Midlands. This was her first job. She had been with the paper for a year. She had completed an NCTJ training course, and done some of her work experience with the same paper. So Tina knew the area quite well, and had developed good local contacts.*

It was one of these who gave her her first big break. And she thought that she might get her story published because the paper had a new editor, one who was not afraid to upset a few local dignitaries in the area.

Her contact was a trade union official working for a large company which manufactured boots. The official had been approached by a friend of his, who was an accountant with the company.

Tina was told only that the man had something important to tell, and that he was afraid to go to the police. She arranged to meet him in a pub some distance from the town where they worked, and it was there that he gave her a possible scoop. The man told her that he could prove that the owner of the company had been fiddling the books. It seemed that the company was in grave financial difficulties, and that the owner was covering up this fact. Worse, he was raising loans to keep the company going on the basis of false information about their trading position. And he was filtering off some of this money into some private account, presumably to insure himself against the inevitable crash. But the accountant was afraid to go to the police because he feared that he would never get another job locally if it was known that he had revealed an employer's secrets, for whatever reason.

He then supplied Tina with enough evidence on paper to support his allegations. She hesitated before going to her editor with the story, thinking that they would have to check their legal position, in any case. But before she could do this, she received an evening telephone call from the company owner himself. The brief conversation certainly proved that she had a possible scandal story on her hands. He told her that if she caused the story to be published or leaked to the police, he would use all his considerable local influence to finish her career as a reporter. Tina knew that, even if the man was later disgraced, this was no idle threat. He could, for example, persuade his friends to bar her from local council meetings and sources of information.

Tina couldn't decide what to do. She went round to see her boyfriend, and they spent a long time talking over the problem, weighing up the problem that she had.

Tina is now a reporter with a national newspaper.

About Tina's story

This tells us something about how and why we use communication to do certain jobs for us. The various means of communication which we have already defined can get things done. When we use them we do so for a reason, with some end in mind, even though we may not be aware of it at the time.

For example, Tina communicates with the union official because she wants to get information. The company owner talks to her because he wants to exert power over her. And she talks to her boyfriend because she wants to make a decision. You may see other reasons why communication takes place in the story. But in all cases it seems that communication is something that is used with a purpose.

3.1   Purpose in communication

All communicating has a purpose.

People must have a reason for communicating. We will look at some of these purposes in the paragraphs below. It is worth remembering that when people communicate, they may be fulfilling more than one purpose at the same time. For example, someone may tell you something that you want to know: their purpose may be to inform you, but at the same time, perhaps, to impress you with their knowledge.

The concept of purpose helps explain what people intend to achieve when they communicate. In our working lives at least, it helps to be clear about our own purposes when we communicate.

Purposes relate to needs in that our purpose is what we intend to get done through communicating in order to satisfy our needs.

Although we may use communication to fulfil more than one purpose at a time, we may not know that we are doing this.

In this sense, **our purposes may be conscious or unconscious**. In the example given above, the person might not be aware that they were 'showing off'. But, by examining how they use words, gesture and tone of voice, we might be able to understand that this was indeed what they were doing. This also makes the point that when we communicate face to face, it is the nonverbal forms of communication which reveal our unconscious purposes.

Similarly **communication may be intentional or unintentional**. If we hurt or upset people through what we say or do, we may not have intended to do this. (Refer back to the comment on intentions at the end of the first section on means of communication, p. 4.) An owl hooting outside a window does not intend to tell me that it is there and that it is night-time. This is not its purpose. So for communication to have purpose, it must (even unconsciously) be directed from one person to another. The people who manufacture a newspaper intend to communicate with their readership. The company which issues a report on its trading over the previous year intends to communicate with its shareholders.

There are several common purposes of communication which are described below:

Information

One basic purpose that we all have in communicating is to give, get or exchange information.

Information is sometimes purely factual. As when ringing up a shop to find out the price of carpets.

But sometimes information cannot strictly be called factual, even though what we get or give does add to the store of knowledge of the other person or of ourselves. For example, if we are interviewing someone, we may try to find out something about their opinions or their attitudes. We are, in a sense, acquiring information about them.

Relationships

Another purpose that we have is to use communication to form or maintain relationships.

There are many kinds of relationship between many kinds of people – friends, work-mates, lovers, parents and children. In a number of cases these involve us with membership of groups. But in all instances we may see that people want to like and be liked, to love and be loved. It is part of our social behaviour that we get together with others, that we want to be part of groups.

Persuasion

People use communication in order to persuade others to think in the way that they do or to act in the way that they do.

The most obvious example of this is advertising. The advertiser intends to persuade a certain category of people – car owners or old age pensioners, for instance – to buy a given product or service. Communication makes the connection with these people persuasively. In the first place, it usually seeks to change the opinions or attitudes of those people regarding the product or service.

However, persuasive communication is more common than we may realize and is not confined to flamboyant examples of advertising. We may want to persuade someone to loan us some money, or to join our drama group, or to help us with repairing our car. It is true that the word 'persuasion' has a certain sense of manipulation – to get what we want. But in this sense we are all manipulators, every day.

Power

Communication can be used with the intention of gaining, maintaining or exerting power over others.

To an extent this may seem to be like persuasion – our purpose is to get someone else to do something we want. But the word 'power' introduces something new into the situation. It suggests that the communicator intends to put the other person in a submissive or helpless position. It can suggest that the communicator has special privileges in terms of what they know or the means of communication that they can use.

For example, a blackmailer has power. This person would possess such significant information about another that we call this other person a victim. If the blackmailer threatens to reveal this information to others, then their purpose in communicating is to exert their power, usually to get money.

Propaganda is communication used to control or manipulate others, usually large groups of people. It involves control of sources of information and of means of communication. This control represents power. The intention is to exert power over the audience. In the 1930s and 1940s, in Nazi Germany, Goebbels' intention in using media was to exert power over the German people by controlling information available to them, and by shaping their beliefs and values.

Mass communications are particularly well suited to this exertion of power because they can broadcast or distribute information and opinion to great numbers of people, from a central source. Those who have power control that central source. By controlling that central source, they have power. That is why there is always concern about who controls the media in any country. The media exert power over their audiences. It is argued that the most important way in which they do this is in respect of shaping people's attitudes and beliefs.

Decision making

We use communication to make decisions about what we think and what we do.

Sometimes decision making is an obvious and calculated activity. For example, the executive committee of a company may have a meeting to make a decision as to whether or not they should build a new factory. All the talk, calculations, plans and other means of communication used at that meeting have to achieve the purpose of making that decision.

But more often, decision making is an unconscious process. So that, indeed, we spend every day making decisions of one sort or another. We may not agonize over whether or not to brush our teeth in the morning, but unconsciously, a quick piece of intra-personal communication goes on inside our heads before we clean our teeth or not.

A more deliberate example of everyday decision making could be one where we have to decide whether or not to go out and see a certain film. It could be that in this case we might ring up a friend and talk it over – see what they know about the film – trying to make our mind up what to do. Our purpose in talking to the friend is to get information and to make a decision.

Self-expression

We use communication to express our imagination and ourselves to others.

This is an important kind of purpose because it covers the creative aspects of communication. We should remember that even in a work situation, communication may be used for more than what are thought of as 'practical' activities.

And this creative expression of the imagination would include the kind of reasoning seen in a book on the possibilities of life existing on other planets, as well as that seen in a television play. What we use our imaginations for covers a wide range of possibilities. One could argue that drawings representing the design concept for a new car show communication being used in the cause of self-expression. And if stories are made through the powers of our imagination then so is our view of ourselves – who we are and what we are like.

In some cases there are such well-established conventions as to how we should dress to express ourselves that we would call them rituals. For example, if we go to a funeral then we wear black. Our purpose is to express a sorrowful state of mind. And the known and set patterns of communication activity on such an occasion turn it into a ritual. By way of contrast, consider the ways we dress and use body language in a different way at a disco. Do you think this is an example of ritual?

Making sense of the world

We use communication to make sense of the world and our experience of it.

We suggest that making sense of the world is about four important things:
- what we believe in,
- what we think of ourselves,
- what we think our relationships are with other people,
- what we think is real.

These ideas map out the physical world, our social world and finally, the world of the mind inside our heads.

So when a child asks questions in order to find out, for example, how Granny is also Mummy's Mummy, he or she is making sense of the world of family relationships. When we watch a television documentary on the life of Australian Aborigines, then we are making sense of another piece of the physical world. And if we become involved in a discussion about the rights and wrongs of the way we treat animals (as when we experiment upon them) – then we are making sense of the world of values and beliefs inside us.

We communicate in order to add to our sense of what the world is like, to check what we believe in, to widen our sense of who we relate to.

Comment

We have suggested seven kinds of purpose, which explain why we use communication. We believe that these cover all kinds of situation. But this is not to say that there aren't other ways of putting it. In fact, it would be useful for you to stop and think of any other ways that you can of explaining our purposes in communicating. Ideas about communicating should always be tested. You should always try to relate the terms used in this book to situations within your own experience.

We are trying to explain what communication is: to describe and interpret it; to explain how and why it happens. This must connect with what you do now, or what you may find yourself doing in the future.

Communication study is about theory and practice, about why we communicate and how we communicate in the ways we do.

4 WHAT HAPPENS WHEN WE COMMUNICATE?

Dave's story

Dave had two things on his mind, and they were bothering him. One was his new job, the other was a new car. He had one but not the other. And he reckoned that the right thing to bring these two items together was a little talk with his bank manager.

It was great having the job – management trainee in a fabrication plant – but it was across town. And besides, they assumed that he would be able to do things like travel to suppliers as part of the training. They had assumed that he had a car when they offered him the job. Or he had let them assume that. Whatever, he hadn't been quite truthful.

But then, he had a licence, so all he needed was the car. And with his increased pay, surely the bank manager would be greeting Dave with several hundred pounds in one hand.

The scenario looked a little grimmer when Dave thought back to his last talk with his bank manager. Not a happy occasion. Still, if he played his cards right. . . .

If he wore his suit, the one he had bought on credit for the job, then that should impress the manager. He should be confident. He could say something like, 'Now look here, Smith. . . .' No, perhaps not . . . something more like, 'Perhaps you could help me, Mr Smith.' Yes, if he cringed enough when he said it, maybe the man would take pity on him. On second thoughts, no cringing. Look him straight in the eye. The trouble was, it was difficult to appear confident when you were actually in that office.

For a start, the guy had two hundredweight of teak desk stuck in front of him. You felt that it was on well-oiled rollers and that all he had to do was to give it a nudge, and the whole thing would come roaring forward to swat you against the wall like a woodlouse under a shoe. Oh well, he would have to play it by ear. See what the man said. Put a straight proposal to him, and see how he reacts. If he starts clicking that rolled gold biro of his, I know I'm dead. Otherwise, we're in with a chance. So long as he's prepared to hear me out.

About Dave's story

One thing you may have noticed about Dave's thinking – he knows that in any communication situation there's quite a lot going on. He was reflecting on what he should say and how he should say it. He was thinking about things like clothes, words, surroundings, all of which are factors in a situation. And when we use more formal words to describe such factors – for example, the surroundings in this case are what we call the physical context, then we are using communication terms to describe what communication is.

And one thing it isn't is still. Once the meeting between Dave and the manager begins, the situation (i.e. the relationship between bank manager and customer) will have to develop. Will Dave move it to the conclusion he wants?

We have already talked about communication being dynamic. Whether we are making the communication or are taking it in, there is something happening. The fact that communication, even reading a newspaper, is an active, doing thing means that we can describe it as a process.

When Dave thought about listening and changing his approach to the bank manager when he saw how the man reacted, he was recognizing that communication is something that 'goes on', especially when people are in face-to-face contact. So let's follow up this idea.

4.1 Communication as a process

When we are in a conversation, there is a continuous exchange going on.

Ideas or facts or opinions are being turned into words and shifted from one person to the other through speech. In chapter 2 we will also look at how, in another part of the process, non-verbal communication is also conveying messages.

So when we talk about the communication process, we are talking about this active flow. **Communication is a process**.

And what we want to do is to explain what's happening, why and how. We want to know what is going on in the process, so that maybe we can improve our handling of it. Through knowledge comes understanding and the possibility of change. So the reason why we look at the communication process from various angles in this book is so that we will become better communicators.

We use communication terms to describe various aspects of the process, breaking it down into stages and parts. We use terms to identify factors which may affect how communication is carried on. We interpret the evidence thus produced and try to make sense of it. Interpretation is not only about making deductions, but also saying why these deductions are significant.

For example, if we see context as a factor in the process, then what is important is to say why it matters in the examples that we are looking at. Theory needs to be applied.

One of the earliest and still the most useful attempts to describe the communication process in separate parts was made by Harold Lasswell in 1948. He said the process of communication could be described in these terms:

Who
says What
in which Channel
to Whom
and with what Effect

Illustration B Communication processes

This is the same as saying that every example of a communication process can be broken down into the following terms:

A Sender
directs a Message
through some Form/Medium
to a Receiver
with some Effect

To these five points could be added at least two more – ideas that we have already suggested.

One is the idea of *context*: because every act of communication must happen in some sort of surroundings. This might be the physical context. It makes a difference as to whether we are trying to talk to someone in a railway station, or in our living room. It might be social context. It makes a difference as to whether we are talking with a group of friends in a pub or with a group of mourners at a funeral.

Another is a double-headed one: the related ideas of *purpose* and *need*. This answers the basic question, why does the communication take place? Everyone has a need that causes them to communicate, and everyone has a purpose in communicating.

So, communication is a process, and this process can be broken down into parts which help explain what is happening, how and why.

When we use certain terms to explain parts of the communication process, we will try to suggest what they mean and give examples. But also remember that there is a glossary near the back of this book which you can use to check out special words.

4.2   Exchange of messages

One dominant idea is that **when we communicate, we exchange messages.**

We give messages and we receive them. These messages are taken into our minds, interpreted, stored or acted upon.

The messages can be about all sorts of things. They could be about something that is happening – a fire in the house next door: or about someone's feelings – they are very unhappy because a relative has just died: or about opinions – we tell someone that we think a certain film is well worth seeing.

In this sense we can also list certain functions of messages (and of the act of communication which puts them across). These functions could be:

to warn,
to advise,
to inform,
to persuade,
to express opinions,
to amuse.

You will recognize some of these words from elsewhere in this chapter. So, rather than our giving you examples this time, see if you can devise word messages which do the sort of jobs we have just listed.

The idea of message, in its broadest sense, is held to cover a wide range of communication forms and media. Maps give us messages about the area of land they depict. Graphs can give us messages about things like the increase in the number of goods which we import into our country. Photographs can give us messages about what people look like in countries that we have never been to. It is even argued that a piece of music is a kind of message from its composer – perhaps about an experience, a mood or feelings.

When we receive such messages we are involved in an exchange process with their makers, just as we are when we make messages ourselves.

Sharing

When we communicate we are also part of a process of sharing.

Communication forms and media carry messages that allow us to share thoughts, feelings, opinions, information and experiences with others. This makes the point that communication, especially in our everyday dealings with others, isn't just about facts. It is about emotions, attitudes and beliefs. These are important to us. They are bound up with the personal and social needs which we have already described.

Such sharing, especially on a personal basis, affects many aspects of our lives, including the time we spend at work. It is all too easy to see work as a business of handling messages of a factual nature. But if our jobs involve dealing with people, then this cannot be the whole truth.

At work, for example, we are frequently concerned about what people think of us, and we of them. We spend time, however briefly, exchanging messages about personal background and experience. Indeed, there is evidence to suggest that how well we deal with 'job messages' depends on how well we are exchanging 'personal messages'.

So sharing is an important aspect of the exchange of messages.

Neutrality of messages

Messages are rarely neutral.

It is possible to argue that simple messages of fact are neutral. For example, a message expressed in word form, such as 'there are two wheels on my motorcycle', seems quite objective.

But then such messages rarely come on their own. In the example just given, there would probably be other verbal and non-verbal messages around that sentence. It would be said in a particular situation and could be said in a particular way. In this case, the speaker could be addressing a friend whose motorcycle is laid up with a smashed front wheel. In that case, the message is not just a statement of fact. It is also saying something like, 'My bike's OK but yours isn't. Hard luck!'

And of course messages in advertisements are never neutral. Even a factual list of functions in a car advertisement is not just a neutral list. It is a selected set of messages about the good points of the car. We don't hear about any possible bad points. We shouldn't be surprised about this lack of neutrality. Any student of communication who examines the purpose behind the message in the communication can see very well why the messages are not neutral.

This isn't to make a moral judgement on the purposes of messages. People may say things with the best of intentions. But we should understand that they do have intentions and are dishonest or unconscious of what they are doing if they say that they don't. This leads on to the idea that messages we exchange may be overt or covert.

Overt or covert messages

Some messages are clear and obvious; some are hidden and not so obvious.

This is another argument for the study of communication. It means that we should look carefully at what is actually being expressed in any example of the communication process.

Sometimes a piece of communication actually intends to hide some of its messages. How good it is at doing this depends on how sharp the receiver is at decoding the communication. For example, an advertisement could be saying overtly, this is a good fabric conditioner which makes your clothes feel soft. But it may also be saying covertly, you aren't a very good mum to your family unless you buy this fabric conditioner. Incidentally, it also conveys opinions about what the advertiser suggests good mums should do!

Sometimes there are hidden messages in a piece of communication which are not intended by the sender. For example, a friend might tell you overtly that she has not been out for the past two weeks and hasn't seen many other friends. What she could be saying covertly is that she is lonely and wants some company.

So there may be more to a piece of communication than is apparent at first glance or at first hearing.

Multiple messages

Communication usually involves the exchange of more than one message at a time.

This is implied by what we have just said. If there are overt and covert messages in a piece of communication, then clearly when we communicate we don't just pass back and forth single, simple messages. Indeed, there is another proposition that goes with this. Communication usually takes place through multiple channels. In the examples given above, we can see that the advertisement probably communicates through pictures and words and the people communicate through speech and non-verbal communication. In fact, where people are concerned, it is often the non-verbal channel which carries the covert messages.

So when we communicate we certainly exchange messages, in the plural.

The nature of messages

We shall discuss messages under the heading of linear models later. But it is worth emphasizing the fact that **messages are not just about what is said. They are about how things are said, and about what channel (or code/codes) is used**.

An American writer, D. K. Berlo, refers to this when he describes the message in three parts: the *code*; the *content*; and the *treatment*.

He also points out that everything we know or experience (including communication from other people) can only enter our consciousness via one or more of the five senses – sight, hearing, touch, taste and smell.

Berlo also refers to the fact that our knowledge, attitudes, communication skills and cultural background affect how we communicate with others. In other words, our effectiveness as communicators depends on what we know, our attitudes, how good we are at communicating and how we have been brought up to communicate.

Whatever happens when we communicate is something that we have learnt to do, in certain ways, for certain reasons.

However, there are other ways of explaining what happens when we communicate.

4.3 Signs and meanings

Communication is all about the giving and receiving of signs which have meanings attached to them.

This is one of the most convincing views of what happens when communication takes place, because it seems to apply to all examples in all situations.

So the idea is that when you speak to someone, you are making signs at them. As long as they know what these signs mean, then they can decode them and the message will have been put across.

The same could be said of any form of communication. A non-verbal sign might be a wink, meaning 'Keep quiet, it's a secret between us.'

A picture sign might be a low camera angle, meaning this person is important and dominating. A musical sign might be a black mark (called a crotchet) which means play this note for a specific length of time. And this page is covered with signs, called letters and words. We hope that they mean something to you.

Meaning

But a sign can only be a sign for us if we assign meaning to it. And there are four problems here:

(a) To say that something is a sign doesn't tell you what its meaning is.
(b) The same sign can have different meanings in different places or at different times.
(c) One sign can have more than one meaning.
(d) The same sign can mean different things to different people.

The answer to the first problem is that **we learn to connect a sign with a meaning**. Mainly, we learn to do this through parents and friends, as part of growing up. We are also taught formally in school. And we should go on learning something about signs and their meanings for the rest of our lives.

If we want to learn the word signs of the spoken French language, then we go on a course where we are taught to make the signs, and are taught to attach meanings to the signs. This second point is important because, of course, being able to say a French word correctly doesn't tell one what it means. Signs are useless unless one knows the meaning. Which is why archaeologists have spent years trying to decipher (decode) some ancient scripts.

The second problem must also be solved by **learning the 'rules' for the right place and the right time**.

Don't tell an American that you want to wash up if you mean that you want to help with the dishes. An American will think that you want to wash yourself. And beware especially of non-verbal signs. You might, as an English person, raise your hand casually, palm outwards, in greeting to someone whom you pass by at work. But for a Greek, the same sign looks suspiciously like an insult! Even within our own culture, we know that putting an arm around someone's shoulders signals different things according to the situation that we are in (and who is involved).

The third problem is obviously connected with the last one. Indeed, the last example could also apply here. But place, time or person don't have to be involved in this case.

Take a written word sign such as 'bow'. As a sign on its own it could refer to the action of bending the body, and an object which projects arrows, and an object which is drawn across the strings of musical instruments. Knowing all the possible means of the sign doesn't help, even though it is a lot better than having no idea at all of what the word means.

From this example we learn that **we often understand the meaning of a sign from other signs around it**. A sentence (string of signs) such as 'She raised the bow and loosed off an arrow at the target', helps pin down the meaning of the word.

Or, to take the example of a party game such as 'charades', we know that the more dress and gesture signs the player gives us, the more likely we are to guess the character being portrayed.

So, if communication is about exchanging signs, or giving and receiving meanings, then the ability to use a wide range and number of signs is likely to aid communication.

The fourth problem may also seem to overlap with the second. But the point is that **even when people are speaking the same language in the same place at the same time, signs can still mean different things**. Take the word 'disgusting'. A dictionary might have us believe that it means something like loathsome or nauseating. But, for example, do parents really mean this when they express their disapproval of the state of their child's room by saying it is disgusting? They probably don't mean that the room actually repulses them. More likely they mean that they disapprove of its untidiness. And if we use a sentence such as – 'It's a disgusting state of affairs when you can't rely on the buses to run on time' – we aren't really talking about physical loathing. We mean that the situation is very annoying and unsatisfactory, so far as we are concerned.

So we really do have to learn a wide variety of possible meanings for signs, and be careful about choosing the meaning which seem to best fit the communicator's intentions. The reverse is also true of course – we must be careful about picking the signs we use, in order to be able to express what we really intend. It is not easy to say what we mean.

Further comment

Just as we may exchange more than one meaning through more than one channel when we communicate, so we may convey more than one meaning through a sign. A glance can express sorrow and regret at the same time.

It may also appear that in some cases we have more than one sign for the same meaning. The sets of words 'naked, nude, starkers' or 'slim, thin, slender' are examples. But in fact, because in the first case the words mean rather more than 'without clothes', one can say that they are not just different signs for the same thing. You work out exactly what they do mean.

Codes

When we communicate through signs we use codes.

A code is a system for using signs. This system is based on rules and conventions shared by those who use the code.

Morse code identifies itself literally. It is a code of long and short electrical signals (dots and dashes) which stand in place of other codes and signs – such as the alphabet and writing, or numbers.

Speech is a series of sound signs which forms a code that we know as spoken words. A photograph of a person represents two forms of communication and two codes. One is the non-verbal code composed of the various dress and body language signs which we see represented in the picture. The other is the pictorial code composed of signs such as de-focused background or close-up on head and shoulders.

The forms and codes of communication are bound by certain 'rules' as to how they are used. These 'rules' are called conventions.

In some instances the conventions are quite strong. One has an organized system of signs. Here the best example is that of spoken or written language. We have all been taught the rules of spelling and grammar: and if we haven't, then we must have learnt them from others. The act of speaking involves knowing which sign goes where. And just as we share knowledge of signs, and more or less agree what they mean, so also we more or less agree on these conventions. Without the organizing power of these conventions, we wouldn't be able to communicate at all. Anyone who mis-pronounces or mis-spells a word badly, fails to communicate that word and so fails to communicate what they mean. And when someone mis-spells a word only slightly and is still understood then it is still the organizing power of those conventions that has saved the day for them and got the meaning across. Because we know how words should be spelt we can work out what a mis-spelt word is probably intended to represent.

Codes are sets of signs. Conventions are rules for using these signs.

It is possible to divide a code into *primary and secondary codes*. A secondary code is a particular form of the primary main code. The primary codes represent the main set of signs for a given form: verbal, non-verbal, pictorial, and so on.

Secondary codes are composed of special sets of signs that work within the primary code. Secondary codes are often related to work (computer talk), or social/sub-cultural groups (bikers). These secondary codes may also have conventions governing their use. We slip into them on many occasions because we think they are appropriate (people baby-talking to young children). Our use of codes is not always appropriate to the occasion or to those present. You might consider the arguments for and against using baby-talk with children as an example.

4.4   Communication as behaviour

This view suggests that the act of communication is a kind of behaviour. It also suggests that we communicate with others in order to modify their behaviour.

The first proposition suggests that communication is as much a kind of behaviour as eating, or banging a nail in a piece of wood. Again, this raises the question of what we know how to do when we are born and what we learn to do afterwards. There are those who think that we learn to do everything after we are born. Others would say that, in the case of speech for example, we are born with a certain *competence* to make speech. Then they would say we develop *performance*, or the skills of speaking.

Either way, there certainly is a lot of learning involved. And it is true that just as we may learn to use a knife and fork or chopsticks to eat with, so we learn to use words in certain ways to put over what we mean, whichever language we may be talking about. And it may be said, just as we learn to behave in different ways according to our upbringing, so **we learn to communicate in different ways according to our upbringing**. So the idea that communication is a kind of behaviour helps us look at why we communicate as we do. If we aren't much good at drawing it could be said that this is because we haven't been taught this particular form of behaviour. Or even if we aren't much good at apologizing to people this is because we haven't learnt much about how to do this.

The second proposition – about modifying the behaviour of others – is easy to understand if, once more, one looks at the example of advertising. Generally speaking, an advertisement wants to change our attitudes so that we then change our behaviour. For example, it might want us to feel favourably disposed towards a certain company's life insurance policy, so that we then go and take out a policy with that company. However, the proposition can be applied to a wider range of examples. For instance, it would be said that a baby cries in a certain way because it has found out that this will cause its mother to give it food. It has changed the mother's behaviour.

The idea that communication changes behaviour doesn't have to be confined to simple examples, where something is seen to happen immediately. It could be said that everything we learn, every piece of information that we acquire changes our behaviour to some extent in the end. Every piece of communication which we experience may affect our attitudes and beliefs in some small way.

We cannot help but change others and be changed by others when we communicate. So, for example, a person might choose a career in social work because he or she had read a publicity booklet which intended to persuade readers that this is a good and worthwhile occupation. On the other hand, someone might choose this career simply because of the many things heard, read or watched about it on television. No one was intending to change this person's attitudes and behaviour. But it happened because of an accumulation of messages.

4.5 Models of communication

Another way of describing the communication process is to use a model.

A model is a medium which is mainly graphic. The parts of the process are laid out, for example to describe what comes first, second, and so on. And the parts are labelled using communication terms. Models are useful because they lay out the process, or a view of what the process is like, in a simple, visual way.

Because there are different terms and different views of what makes up the communication process, so there are different models.

And one can change the terms of a communication model without changing the layout. For example, we can talk in general terms about the receiver of a message, whatever the situation. But in fact, if we were referring to receivers of music at a concert or receivers of a radio programme, then it is more appropriate to use the term 'audience'. And this is what models for mass communication tend to do. They do this because the term 'audience' draws attention to the fact that there is often more than one receiver for a piece of mass communication, and to the fact that such receivers are not engaged in the communication process in the same way as people talking face to face.

Models and the terms used in models may be changed to emphasize particular points about a situation – i.e. the difference between making a speech or reading a book.

There are a variety of models used in this and other books. You will find some models worked out by other people useful. But remember that communication studies is about doing. Be prepared to make up your own models. Models can be more or less complicated, according to the number of terms used, and the ingenuity of the layout.

We will start with the most simple style of model.

Linear models

These lay out parts of the process in a line, as if communication is all about sending messages from A to B. In fact, communication is rarely that simple, but it is a good enough way to begin. This model, shown in figure 1, with a simple situation indicated below it, suggests a few terms and ideas.

Source and *destination* make the point that communication always comes from someone and goes to someone. But it matters as to who exactly the source and destination are. For example,

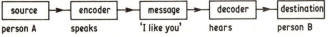

Figure 1   Basic linear model of communication

one would want to take into account whether person B is male or female.

The idea of *codes* has been described on p. 29. Communication has to be expressed through some form or medium and these all have their own codes. For example, the message above could have been encoded through a non-verbal sign, such as touching. This is a different code from that of speech. In any case thoughts or feelings have to be expressed in some form to be 'decoded' and understood by someone else.

And then there is the term *message* – what is said, or expressed one way or another. As we have said, D. K. Berlo has broken this term down into three parts: content, code and treatment. In the example given above, the content is 'I like you', the code is that of speech and the treatment depends on how it is said – warmly, lovingly, factually, and so on.

Exchange models

These indicate that communication is at least a two-way process.

In the case of a group of people, it may seem to be more than two-way. In the case of someone watching television it may be difficult to see how there is a response to the messages coming from the television set. This will be discussed in the last chapter of the book. But for situations discussed in chapter 2, this kind of model, shown in figure 2, is very useful. This model makes the point that messages go both ways in a conversation. It also says that everyone is a decoder and an encoder. That is to say, we have to find some way of putting together and expressing what we have to say, as well as some way of taking in what the other person says.

But then, we also have to make sense of what is said. This is where the term 'interpreter' comes in. We are all interpreters of messages, all day and every day. How we interpret messages is another matter. This will be discussed later. But we will find that there are reasons why people may interpret the same message in different ways. Here is a fundamental reason for studying communication. If we all got our messages across exactly as we intended, there would be fewer problems between people. But this doesn't happen. When we examine the idea of perception, we will see that because we all have different kinds of experience, and make different kinds of assumption, so we interpret messages in different ways.

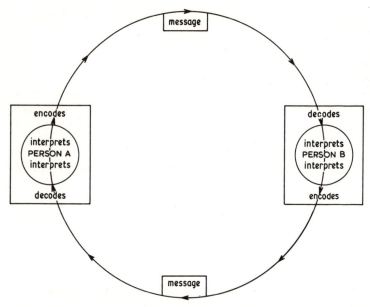

Figure 2   An exchange model of communication

Sometimes the difference isn't great. Sometimes it is, and it matters.

For example, looking back to the situation of the first model, if the person who is the source of the message (person A) is female and the person who is the destination (person B) is male, and if person B interprets the message as loving when it was meant to be just friendly, then the two people concerned have got problems. We will return to examples of problems throughout this book.

Contextualized models

These models add the dimension of situation or surroundings.

This matters more or less to how communication takes place according to the particular example. But **context always affects the act of communication**.

For example, we would communicate differently in the situation of a formal dinner party with our boss, as compared with eating fish and chips in the kitchen with friends. This example shows that context has both physical and social aspects.

Figure 3 is a model which includes context. One other term is important.

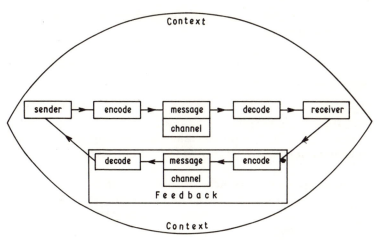

Figure 3 Linear model of communication with context and feedback

This new term is *feedback*. It reminds us that communication is often two-way: that there are responses to messages sent. And that we adjust the way that we carry on a conversation, for example, according to the feedback that we get from the other person. The channel which conveys feedback does not have to be speech but may be non-verbal – for example a bored expression or a movement of the feet in readiness to leave.

You will also notice that we have changed the words 'source' and 'destination' in figure 1 to 'sender' and 'receiver'. You may come across these terms in other books. Try to decide for yourself which words are most useful.

CONCLUSION

We have argued that **the act of communication is one in which meanings are exchanged through signs**. We have made a number of suggestions about what happens when we communicate. And explaining what happens when we communicate helps explain what communication is.

Generally, in this chapter we have given ways of:

explaining why we communicate,

describing how we communicate.

Now you can check what we have said by looking at the summary which follows. After that, we suggest a number of activities which will bring out some of the points we have made, and which will encourage you to check our ideas and explanations as to what communication is.

REVIEW

This is to help you check on the main points of this first chapter, 'What is communication?'

First we said that communication is something that we experience in various ways. So then we asked ourselves:

1 How do we experience communication?

1.1 Through various means of communication which you should be able to define and give examples of, from the list that follows:

forms,
medium,
the media,
other kinds.

1.2 As a connection between people, joining friend with friend, or newspaper reporter with newspaper reader.

1.3 As an activity, because it is something that we do. We make communication in order to make things happen in our lives.

1.4 As something which we have learnt to do, like other skills and abilities which we have.

1.5 Within four main categories of communication activity. Again, you should be able to define and give examples of these from the list that follows:

intrapersonal communication,
interpersonal communication,
group communication,
mass communication.

Second, we said that there has to be a reason for communicating to take place. So then we asked the question:

2 Why do we communicate?

to satisfy needs that we have within us,
to survive, physically and as social beings,
to feel secure and valued by others,
to be involved with others, in relationships,
to conduct the everyday business of our lives,
to give and receive information,
to play with ideas and stories.

Third, we said that communication does things for us. So then we asked the question:

3   What do we use communication for?
we want to give and get information,
we want to form or maintain relationships,
we want to persuade others,
we want to gain, maintain or exert power,
we want to make decisions,
we want to express ourselves and our imagination,
we want to make sense of the world.

Fourth, we said that it is possible to break down what actually happens when we communicate, in terms of how it is done and what affects it. So then we asked the question:

4   What happens when we communicate?

4.1   We are involved in a process in which many things are happening at the same time. The process can be broken down into various parts, according to a given situation, which can be described through special terms.

4.2   We exchange messages, which may be about facts, opinions or beliefs. This means that we share information, feelings and ideas with others. But we have to take account of the fact that messages are rarely neutral, that messages may be overt or covert and that messages are usually multiple (more than one is exchanged at a time). The term 'message' can be divided into three parts: content, code and treatment.

4.3   We are giving and receiving signs and their meanings but signs can have more than one meaning: they mean different things to different people; they change their meaning according to time and place; and meanings only belong to a sign because we agree that they do. Together the signs in a form of communication make up codes. These codes depend on conventions which govern how they are used, which we learn and which help the communication to make sense.

4.4   We are involved in a kind of behaviour which may well be a way of trying to change the behaviour of others.

4.5   We can see this process very clearly through the use of models. These fall into various types. You should be able to define and give examples of the following types:
linear,
exchange,
contextualized.

ACTIVITIES

In each case, we suggest that these can be undertaken by individuals, pairs or groups. Many of these activities can be performed by individuals if preferred. But we believe in the value of discussion and collaboration where communication tasks are concerned.

1   For pairs or groups.
To illustrate the concept of need.

Take two situations in which communication must take place. In the first case the situation involves an 18-year-old who has got a job and intends to leave home. This person has to explain things to his or her parents.

In the second case a firm specializing in graphics work has to design a pack of safety stickers to be used in the kitchen for warning children against danger from appliances.

Now list the needs for communication which you think must be satisfied in each case. Explain differences of need between the two situations, if any.

2   For individuals and pairs.
To examine the concepts of source, audience and purpose.

Take four examples of means of communication:
  (a) a charity appeal advertisement,
  (b) a page from a child's comic,
  (c) a driving licence application form,
  (d) a photograph from a family album.

Describe the source, audience and purpose of the communication in each case. Comment on similarities and differences.

3   For individuals or pairs.
To illustrate the significance of role, relationship, context and media in the communication process.

Take these three situations:
  (a) a wireless operator putting out a mayday distress call from a ship,
  (b) a father playing with a 2-year-old child,
  (c) two prisoners in adjoining cells exchanging messages.

Design a communication model for each which includes some or all of the terms listed above. Say why you put in or leave out terms.

Compare your use of terms in each case.

4   For groups.
To illustrate the importance of signs, meanings and conventions.

  (a) How would you explain the meanings of 'hair', 'here', 'hare', 'hear' to someone who doesn't speak English very well?

(b) Produce a set of package signs for the following types of goods: fragile goods, heavy goods, liquid goods, perishable goods.

(c) Compose the following 'rule breaking' (convention breaking) pictures by cutting up and remounting existing photographs and/or by drawing to illustrate the following:
  (i) a pirate queen,
  (ii) a trendy grandfather,
  (iii) a poor bank manager.
  Remember to place them in a context if you can.

Discuss your choice of signs to construct these meanings, as well as the conventions that you think have been broken.

SUGGESTED READING

Myers, T. M., and Myers, E. G., *The Dynamics of Human Communications*, chapters 1, 2 and 5.

Schramm, W., *Men, Women, Messages and Media*, chapters 1–6.

Fiske, J., *Introduction to Communication Studies*, introduction and chapters 1–4 (but be warned that some of this is written for an advanced level).

See also the resources list at the end of this book for further details of these and other books.

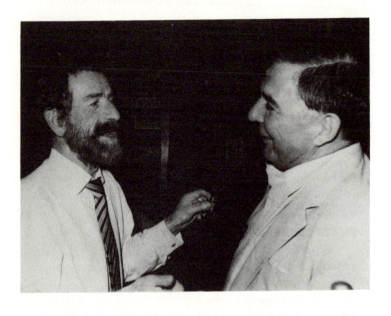

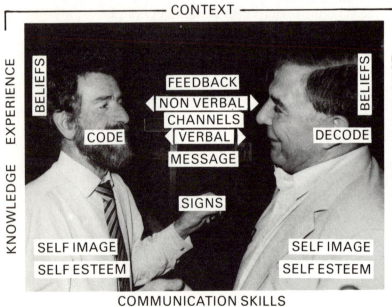

Illustration C Interpersonal communication analysed

·2· INTERPERSONAL COMMUNICATION

'Communication is essentially a social process.'
(Colin Cherry, *World Communication: Threat or Promise?* 1978)

This chapter provides information about communication between individual people. It includes accounts of how speech and non-verbal communication enable us to relate to one another. There is also comment on how we present ourselves to others, how we perceive other people, and on barriers to communication.

---

1 MEANS OF CONTACT

Hazel's story

The Spanish beach was crowded and as hot as a warm bath. Hazel tipped her straw hat back a little. The cries of children sounded like complaining seagulls. Only there weren't any seagulls around this beach. Hazel shifted position on her beach towel and opened one eye. There wasn't even the noise of the cicadas which could usually be heard scraping away. It was too hot and too near the town for them. Hazel opened the other eye, wide. The children were gone.

She sat up abruptly. Ten minutes ago Laura and Tim had been playing at the water's edge, in a straight line with her big toe. Hazel scanned along the water line anxiously. Surely they must be all right. After all, Laura was 6 years old and Tim was 8. And two kids can't go far in ten minutes or less. She looked around the encampments filling the beach. A dark haired, handsome youth grinned at her, encouragingly. Hazel scowled at him. Another time, Don Juan, she thought.

Panic began to set in when she stood up and still saw no familiar blond heads. Pauline and Roger will go mad, she thought. I'll murder those kids. Aunty Hazel is not going to be popular.

Within twenty-five minutes she was at the local police station and wishing that she had learnt some Spanish before they came on this holiday. Luckily, someone had helped her on the way, when she was trying to find the word for 'police'. That, and some determined gestures had got her to the right place. But the kids were still missing. And she felt silly, clutching a striped beach bag and with only a beach robe over her bikini.

The Spanish policeman who was trying to help her was courteous and charming. But he didn't speak any English. Hazel tried a few simple words and then gave up, as they smiled at one another uncomprehendingly. There was plenty of good will on both sides, but that was all at the moment. Hazel wished that her brother-in-law was there. He spoke a little Spanish. Even the word for 'child' would be a help. Something had to be done. She was beginning to believe that something terrible could have happened to the children. Perhaps she should just go back to the beach and wait.

Hazel looked the policeman in the eye and took a deep breath. She made a flat handed gesture, with her palm, about the height of Laura's head from the floor. Then she shrugged her shoulders and tried to look anxious. The policeman looked on with interest and then pointed suddenly to a picture on the wall. It was a photograph of a child.

About Hazel's story

This tells us about the different ways of making contact with other people. We tend to take things like words and gestures for granted – until they don't work the way we want them to. These verbal and non-verbal forms of communication are in fact the channels through which we pass messages to others. Most of us have forgotten the experience of early years, when we were learning the signs which belong to these forms, and what they mean. It is only when we are stuck in a situation like Hazel's that we may rediscover what it was like to be a young child, cut off from others, without means of contact. But, even a young child who cannot speak still has some ways of getting through to others. Hazel got through to the policeman when she smiled at him, and when she used her body and her hands to express what she meant. For interpersonal communication to happen, there must be some means of contact with the other person. There are two principal means of contact: non-verbal communication and speech.

1.1 Non-verbal communication (NVC)

We make and receive non-verbal signs whenever we are with others.

These signs are not words, but they are often used with words. They affect the meaning of what we say. They are produced by various uses of our bodies, by the way we dress ourselves and by the ways in which we can utter the words which make up speech. They say a lot about our feelings and our attitudes towards others. And they can be used apart from words. We become well aware of this when a policeman raises his hand to stop our car at a junction, or if an angry driver waves his fist at us.

These non-verbal signs can be placed under three main headings: (a) body language; (b) paralanguage; (c) dress.

(a) Body language

This tells us a lot about people's *feelings, attitudes and intentions*. Actors understand this very well when they put on non-verbal signs in order to convince the audience of the part that they are playing. Some books try to convince their readers that the key to success with the opposite sex lies in the use of non-verbal signs. This is only partially true. People may like us if we are pleasant and friendly towards them: and a lot of this friendliness is shown through body language. But it is not the only thing that matters. There are a great many signs that we give off when we are talking to someone. It is the meaning of all of these together which counts. And meaning varies according to the situation and who is involved. Having said this, it is also true that we are capable of paying more attention than we do to what other people are saying to us through their body language. And we are capable of controlling our body signs more carefully than we do, so that, for example, we get on with people better. In other words, our communication skills are learnt, and we can learn more. In which case it is useful to have some idea of what we are doing.

Body language includes five main elements, as follows:

(i) **Gesture:** the way we use our arms and hands.

It is common to see people wave across a crowded room to attract attention, and then beckon someone to them. We use gesture to express things like height and width of objects we are describing. But there are more subtle signs, such as the steepling of fingers to express confidence. And for some people, gestures are part of their job – the tic-tac men at a race-course, signalling bets and results. There are some complete languages of gesture – codes: so-called 'deaf and dumb' language, for example.

(ii) **Expression:** the way that we signal with our faces.

This usually says a lot about mood and emotion. The eyes and the mouth dominate expression signs. These are the signs which people look for first when they are trying to weigh up someone. We are capable of distinguishing subtle variations in smile or look. If someone gazes at you a lot, then it means they are interested in you. If two people gaze at one another a lot then it means that they have a positive and trusting relationship. Or again, we are able to distinguish between the raised eyebrow of surprise, of fear or of acknowledgement when we meet a friend. In short, we do a lot of looking during the process of encoding and decoding body signs.

(iii) **Body posture:** the way that we hold our bodies.

A relaxed posture expresses confidence in the person whom we are talking to. On the other hand, at an interview you would be well advised to sit up straight and look interested! To take another example, when one talks about a confrontation, it means just that. Bodies positioned front to front. Together with closeness and direct gaze, this signals mutual aggression. So it isn't surprising to find that, in the west at least, people normally stand with their bodies slightly averted from one another, when having a conversation. This is considered polite. It signals that your intentions are friendly or neutral.

(iv) **Body space and body proximity:** how near to others we stand or sit.

First, everyone needs a certain space around them, to feel comfortable. Factors such as the age or the sex of people involved in an exchange can make a difference to this. But generally, adults won't let another person get within arm's reach unless they know them pretty well. Indeed, one can guess the degree of people's friendship from the way that they treat each other's body space. It may be possible to get on good and friendly terms with someone by 'dipping' into their body space. But it is advisable to think hard about the person and the situation because this may also upset them. This is when one starts talking about body proximity. People often rate their status according to proximity. So, while it may be all right to get close to friends and loved ones, the boss may take a dim view of what could be seen as 'familiarity'. The meaning of body proximity, like that of other non-verbal signs, varies from culture to culture.

(v) **Touch:** is about who we touch, when, where and how.

It tells us a lot about relationships, status and degrees of friendliness. Women tend to do more touching with women, just as young children do more touching than adults. But obviously there are all kinds of special situations with special rules, such as those concerning lovers. It is also notorious that the British are one of the least 'touching' nations in the world, which can provide serious problems in our relationships with those from other cultures. There is some evidence that more touching – within the broad social rules – would help us get on better with others, including those from our own culture. Usually, when we are touched (however briefly) by the other person, during an interaction, then we feel more friendly towards them. Sales people have been known to exploit this reaction.

(b) Paralanguage

This tells us a lot about how to interpret the meanings of words during a conversation. It describes the non-verbal signs which accompany speech. There are those signs which are separate from the words themselves.

They are often about immediate reactions and emotions. We may whistle or gasp in surprise. People making public speeches are fond of 'er' and 'um', which is really a sign for 'Hold on, I'm thinking up the next bit.' We may scream with fright or groan with pain.

There are those signs which are represented through ways in which the words themselves are pronounced. They are signs such as pitch, stress and volume. We don't speak like robots in a flat and even way. So when the voice rises at the end of a sentence, for example, it may tell us that this is a question. Try delivering this set of words as a statement and as a question and you will see what we mean – 'You'll meet me at eight o'clock tonight.' Another example of this kind of paralanguage is to be seen in the fact that we often know that a person is angry when they begin speaking loudly. And again, it would be impossible for people to be sarcastic or speak ironically without the aid of these special signs.

Paralanguage can suggest things about a person's state of mind or their emotions. When we say that a person is calm or excitable or nervous, then it is the way that they deliver their words which can tell us this. So if we want to present ourselves well at an interview, then we could try to use the calm and even tones of someone who is confident and who is thinking about what they are saying. At the same time, we would try not to speak in a flat, monotonous manner, because that would suggest that we are boring or bored.

(c) Dress

The third kind of non-verbal communication that we use is to do with dress, hair, jewellery and make-up.

This one says a lot about personality, role, job and status. For example, characters in television comedy and advertisements are given certain kinds of dress to make them easily identified. An extrovert type may be given wild and colourful hair, with bright clothes. Housewives are put in aprons. Stockbrokers wear dark jackets and pin-stripe trousers. And important people are seen in a Rolls-Royce, wearing expensive clothes.

You could try making your own analysis of the dress of a police woman, a priest, a nurse and a teacher.

Dress also signals people's identity. When we group people by class or job (soldier) or sub-culture (punks), often it is clothes which first identify them with the group.

Comment

NVC has a number of characteristics and functions. Some functions occur when it is used with language. For example, it may reinforce something that is being said, as when a speaker chops one hand down upon the other in an emphatic gesture. Or it may elaborate on what is said when, for example, a speaker uses a level hand palm down to add to a description of the height on a child. Sometimes a non-verbal sign can have the function of modifying what is said. For example it is possible to smile at someone at the same time as 'telling them off'. The smile takes the edge off the spoken disapproval.

NVC is a primary code of communication, as much as written language. It also has its share of secondary codes. For example, the floor manager of a television production has a special set of signs by which he communicates with programme presenters.

NVC is also controlled by conventions (rules) in the way it is used. These conventions are not as exact as the rules of grammar, which control our use of language. But they do make it probable that, for example, we will look at someone just before we smile, just before we shake hands with them.

Ritual kinds of non-verbal behaviour are also common. Chanting and flag-waving fans at the football match every Saturday show this. Some rituals are well known and public, such as those in a church service. But others may be less obvious, if no less a matter of habit. See if you can think of any examples of ritual NVC which you know of, at home, at school, at work.

Non-verbal cues may be involuntary or intentional. Signs such as blushing are considered to be reflexes which we can't control. It is in fact quite difficult to control many non-verbal signs. But it can be done to an extent – politicians practise such control for their public appearances. It is an interesting question as to whether NVC is intentional or not. We learn to use the signs subconsciously in most cases, yet they are not produced by accident, and so it would seem that there is some intention there to communicate. Perhaps we should all try to be more conscious of what our intentions are.

NVC is specific to nations or cultures. A culture or sub-culture is a collection of people who have strong beliefs and values in common. They may have a certain religion, recognizable arts of their own, what we would call a way of life of their own. Cultures can often cut across national boundaries, as is the case with Jewish people. Cultures can exist within nations, as is the case with West Indian communities in Britain.

Television and travel have helped carry non-verbal signs (and words) across national boundaries in the world today, so that people are tempted to think that gestures and expressions mean the same everywhere. Not so. One may see the same signs in other places, but they don't necessarily mean the same thing as they do in Britain.

Even though a very few signs are used quite widely, such as the lifted eyebrow flash to express surprise, many other signs do not travel well. Men from Middle Eastern cultures like to stand close and face the person whom they are talking to. Men from western cultures don't like this directness and closeness so they are inclined to dance away from an Arabic speaker, who of course quicksteps after them in order to show what he considers to be polite signs of conversation.

Precisely because this is an age of international travel, we should think about our NVC as much as our words when on holiday or business abroad.

So NVC is a complex combination of signs through which we can communicate even when we aren't talking. They give rise to the proposition that we cannot help communicating, whether we like it or not. So, whatever clothes you put on, other people will be noting these, and to some extent, trying to read something into them.

NVC relates to our perception of others (section 4 of this chapter). A significant part of what we perceive in others is in their non-verbal signs.

NVC helps build and maintain relationships. Because non-verbal signs say a lot about our attitudes towards one another, so they influence the nature of our relationships. Positive relationships depend on positive attitudes. These attitudes can only be understood through appropriate uses of NVC.

NVC relates to the idea of feedback (section 3 of this chapter). We give off and make sense of these signs very rapidly indeed, even at the same time as we are talking or listening. So it is hard to 'notice' everything that is going on. This is where it is useful to look at videotape recordings of people in conversation and slow them down, so that one can see just how the people involved are signalling to one another.

For example, in an interview one could look at several units of interaction. In the first place there is the 'handshake' procedure, when the two people greet one another. Then there is the period of initial assessment where usually insignificant questions are asked, but the two people are weighing each other up in terms of personality and attitude. And then there is a period of evaluation, where as well as handling a question-and-answer session on a verbal level, the two people are checking and confirming (or not) their first impressions of each other, on a non-verbal level. And there is plenty of evidence that non-verbal impressions can strongly influence the outcome of an interview.

1.2   Speech

We have already seen that there is more to conversation than the acts of delivering and hearing words.

The exact meaning of what we say depends on our use of paralanguage in particular. And of course other non-verbal signs accompany the words. A fist in the palm of the hand may help emphasize the importance of what we are saying. On the other hand, a mocking smile may accompany an apparently pleasant remark: it could contradict what we said, and point to an opposite, true meaning.

Spoken words are sound signs. We have a tendency to regard words as somehow natural and true, as if they are an absolute fact of life. In our last story, Hazel found out that this certainly isn't true, when she realized that she couldn't make the right sounds to communicate with the policeman. Actually words themselves are made up of small units of sound called phonemes. We combine these to make a spoken word, and that word is only a sign. The fact that the signs mean something to us is the result of a long process of learning. The word 'dog' could just as well be the word 'bart'. If everyone thought of the same animal when the sound 'bart' was uttered, then it would do just as well as 'dog'.

And, as with other cases that we have looked at, we often need more than one of these sound signs to work out what they actually mean. For example, for most people, the spoken words 'there' and 'their' and 'they're' all sound pretty much the same. Try saying them. It is only when they are uttered *in the context* of a sentence that we can be sure of which one is meant.

Speech is a code of signs, ruled by conventions. This follows what we have previously said. Many other forms of communication, such as NVC and pictorial images (film and photographs), consist of codes. The rules by which these codes are used are called conventions.

We expect words to appear in a certain order (called syntax) and to be combined in a certain way to produce 'proper' English (called grammar). What we call the English language is a primary code of communication. We learn its signs and conventions at an early age because it satisfies a lot of our basic human needs to be able to speak. We will also learn some of its secondary codes and their conventions because they also have special uses. For example, air traffic controllers and airline pilots have their own code within the main code of English, which uses special words in special ways. People who haven't learnt their code can't understand them.

Dialect is also an example of a code. It represents regional differences from 'standard' English. These differences are to do with vocabulary, or the collection of words that one uses, as well as to do with the ways in which those words are used. A common example is the shifting of pronouns, where a dialect speaker might say 'I' instead of 'me'. There are many examples of dialect words in use. In the west of England, where we are writing this book, people often talk about 'daps', where others might talk about gymshoes, or even plimsoles. Dialect is not improper English. It is another version of English. In a given region it may be the main spoken language code in use. Many people use more than one code anyway: standard and dialect. The reason that it is useful to be able to use 'standard' English is that it does provide a good chance that one will be clearly understood by English speakers wherever one may be.

Accent should not be confused with dialect. Certain accents may go with certain regional codes, but accent is part of the sign system of paralanguage. Everyone has an accent. It says a lot about our beliefs and values, especially with relation to class, that many people are brought up to think that there is a middle class which has no accent and that this is 'normal' and 'proper'. This is purely a matter of opinion. English people who have not been brought up to distinguish the relevant signs have no idea what a proper Scottish accent should be. The idea of 'proper' is just a meaning which we have chosen to associate with certain signs.

Speech uses register. This follows on from our last point. We have the ability to choose our speech from two kinds of broad code, labelled upper and lower register. The distinction is usually thought of in terms of the difference between ordinary English and 'posh' English. In fact, once more this is a rather snobbish way of looking at it. Upper register is simply a rather more careful kind of English with a wide vocabulary and formal syntax, which we would use when we want to be careful about what we say – for example, if we were giving evidence in court. Self-conscious use of upper register sounds strained and silly: for example, the policeman in the same court who is 'proceeding in a northerly direction', instead of walking down the road to where it meets the High Street. The point is that we need this careful upper register when we have to explain things accurately or argue things through logically. That is all. It is no good saying 'Put a bit of the yellow liquid in the brown stuff' when trying to explain something to a trainee in the laboratories of a chemical company. The result could be a bang!

To take another example, we might well use lower register to chat about a training film that we had seen as part of our job. But if we had to give an oral report on it to our supervisor, then we would probably shift into upper register, for the appearance of accuracy and objectivity.

Speech uses idiom and colloquialisms. It isn't necessary to have an English language lesson to be able to analyse and use spoken communication more effectively. But it is useful to have labels for some of the more common ways of handling language. Colloquialisms are the characteristics of everyday, casual speech. They appear in lower register use. Simple examples are 'won't' and 'can't' for 'will not' and 'can not'.

Idiom refers to some of the slangy and more grammatically inaccurate ways in which we use everyday speech. The sort of things that make it hard for people from other countries to learn English. We know what we mean when we tell someone to 'belt up!', but it is an odd thing to say if you think about it from the point of view of, say, a German.

Speech is part of culture. That is to say, we develop the kind of spoken language which expresses the things our culture believes in, its ideas, even just the objects with which it is familiar. This is why translating from one language to another is so hard. The French, for example, don't have exactly the same set of ideas and objects as we do, with merely a different code of sound signs. They talk about 'ennui': we translate it as 'boredom'. But this isn't exactly what it means to them. It also says something about tiredness of the spirit. More obviously, it is hardly surprising to find that Eskimos have many different words for different kinds of snow. They need them in a land where their lifestyle and their very survival depends on different kinds of snow.

If the study of communication is a study of how we produce meanings from signs, then we should be aware that culture affects this process, and that spoken language helps define the culture. What people mean when they say something depends partly on their background, and their culture is very much part of this background. Because there are cultural variations within what we broadly call English culture, we can come up against problems even in one country. For a start, there is the question of our so-called racial minorities. Someone whose background is Pakistani and who is being interviewed for a job may feel it necessary to say a lot about their qualifications. Their use of English might be 'good', but their intention and meaning would be subtly different from that of the average English person. In their sub-culture, it is a matter of status and sound argument at an interview to stress good qualifications. The English interviewer would see this as slightly irrelevant and a little boastful. In this example, the cultural factor does matter. Also, different people from different backgrounds in different parts of one country may represent cultural variations. They may use language slightly differently, or mean different things by it. People often talk about the differences between the north and south of England. What are these differences? Are they to be seen in the use of spoken language?

Comment

Speech has particular uses. It is true that various forms of communication can be used in various ways to satisfy a variety of needs. But it is also true that particular forms are better at doing some things than others. Photographs are good at representing visual aspects of the world. Speech is not so good in this respect – though no doubt students of descriptive and creative writing would object to this remark!

However, spoken language is very good at dealing with ideas, opinions and arguments – what we call abstracts; things to do with the world of the mind, as opposed to a physical and material world. Speech is quick, immediate, flexible, a form of communication that everyone has some ability to use and which doesn't require assistance from technology – not even a pen! Our relationships depend on speech because we have made it a tool for describing and discussing feelings. Our sciences depend on speech because we have made it a tool for explanation and reasoning. Words allow us to suggest things that might happen, but haven't: to discuss things that have happened, but aren't happening any more. All aspects of our working and social lives depend on being able to use words. But best of all they allow us to reason and to deal with feelings.

This is not to discount the value of other forms and codes, but if you make a list of the things that you use speech for in a day, then you may appreciate the special importance it has in the process of communication.

2 MAKING CONTACT

Steve's story

The phone rang again and Steve picked it up.
'Hallo. Perry Travel Agency. Can I help you?'
There was a giggle on the other end of the line.
'Madeleine! Er – what's wrong?'
'Nothing. And you don't have to whisper.'
'OK, I'm sorry. But you know they don't like calls in working hours.'

'Suppose it was something important? Suppose I was pregnant?'
'You aren't!'
'Well, I'm not telling you now.'
'Come on, Maddy. Be fair, I'm expecting a call from Heathrow.'
'All right. Well – I thought I ought to let you know. I've finally got through to my mother. It's all right to go down there on Saturday. I thought I'd tell you so that you don't let them con you into coming in this Saturday, after all.'

Steve took a deep breath. He liked to play golf and had fixed up a match with some friends only that morning. He thought about playing for time, but opted for the direct approach instead.

'Maddy, there's one slight problem. . . .'
'Steve, with you there are no slight problems. But if you planned to make me a golf widow again, then nothing doing. You said you would go down to Holmelea.'
'Yes. But you hadn't got anything fixed up when I left this morning. And it's Thursday already.'

There was a click as Madeleine put down the receiver. Steve bit his nails distractedly. Now what was he going to do? They had all paired up for Saturday. He was going to be really popular if he pulled out now. On the other hand, he had already upset Madeleine. And he had agreed to go and see her mother. Steve groaned and Miss Hobbs looked up, startled. He smiled reassuringly.

It was no good. Golf would have to go. He couldn't win either way, but he couldn't upset Madeleine. Wives before friends . . . or something like that. The question was how to make excuses to the others. He'd have to lead in to it gently, then have some good reason, and top it all off with a generous lashing of apologies.

Steve began to make a list of possible excuses on his jotter pad. The phone rang.

'This is Sabena calling from Heathrow. You asked about a flight. . . .'

About Steve's story

This tells us that interpersonal communication is concerned with making contact with others, either directly or by using some technology such as the telephone, which helps link person to person. So far, we have concentrated on talking about means of communication. Speech, like the telephone, is a tool to do a job. How we use these tools is another matter. In this section we want to look at various ways in which we do make contact with others.

Steve's case is a fairly typical example of contact, in that it is within a relationship and is, in a sense, about that relationship. He has to deal with a minor problem in his personal life.

We do a lot of talking in our lives and much of that talk is concerned with people. We have ways of talking – or of contacting others. The way that we talk and use NVC isn't accidental. We learn signs and meanings. We learn how to manipulate signs and meanings. Steve was planning a piece of manipulation when he was reflecting on how he would explain to his friends that he couldn't play golf with them after all. He was in fact planning a communication strategy.

2.1 Strategies

A strategy is a short piece of communication behaviour or interaction. It involves the deliberate use of verbal and non-verbal signs to achieve a communicative purpose.

We use these strategies the whole time, though we may not be aware of it. One of the earliest and most simple strategies that a baby uses, for example, is the hunger cry. What starts off as a reflex becomes a deliberate yell for food, and then perhaps for attention. The child learns to generate communication signs deliberately.

Salespersons are actually taught strategies for dealing with people so that they stand a better chance of making a sale. In effect, this involves learning a set of verbal and non-verbal signs which, it is hoped, will have the desired effect. So, among other things they may be taught to do a lot of smiling, to find excuses (such as the use of brochures) for getting inside the client's body space, to refer to details of the client's lifestyle or home approvingly, to agree (or to appear to agree) with everything the client says, to relate their product or service to the client's known or supposed needs. All this proves that communication can be controlled, can be used for an effect – whether or not we approve of what the effect is. And it comes about as a result of using one or more strategies.

Of course, not all strategies are persuasive. You might consider what you think people do when they use strategies for encouraging a child in its reading or for comforting a woman whose husband has been injured in a traffic accident.

We use the most common strategy every day in its various forms. This is the 'greetings strategy'. A strategy doesn't have to be a lengthy piece of interaction. Greetings can be quite short.

But still, what happens is that various non-verbal signs and words are used to show that the people involved recognize one another, feel friendly towards one another, and confirm the nature of their relationship.

Some strategies, like the greetings ones, can become a matter of habit. If the same pattern of communication is used again and again then it becomes a ritual. Some strategies are used more consciously than others. Obviously, if we are not familiar with a given situation then we have to think more consciously about what strategy is most useful. But once a general type of strategy has been tried once, then it is easier to think up variations on it. For example, pupils have quite a stock of useful excuses for being late for school, from 'The bus came early' to 'The cat was sick on my school bag'. But the basic strategy remains the same – it always includes elements such as the breathless arrival, the sincere, direct gaze and the verbal apology.

There are a great number of strategies that we do use, so many that it is hard to categorize them. One way of doing so is to look at communication needs as mentioned in chapter 1, and place all strategies under one of these headings. Other ways of describing strategies have already been mentioned, in effect, through examples in this section. So, we have strategies for persuading, for approving or disapproving, for making excuses and for avoiding people and problems.

Finally, one very common set of strategies that we have is to do with conversation. One could say this is the basic stuff of every-day interpersonal communication, but again, conversations don't just happen and develop by chance. We communicate because we want to. We use strategies to shape conversation. The most common ones are these: starting and finishing a conversation; interrupting people; keeping the conversation going; changing the direction of the conversation.

All these strategies may happen quite quickly, but still, the signs achieve the purpose. For example, in the case of interrupting we may use a sign such as a small cough to distract the speaker, we will use eye contact and perhaps a small finger movement to say that we are ready to speak, and we may nod our head vigorously to signal that we have taken in what the previous speaker has to say, and that he or she can now shut up!

2.2   Presentation of self

We present different personalities to other people according to the situation we are in.

The idea that we present ourselves to others in different ways at different times comes from a book by Erving Goffman. It provides a useful and entertaining account of how we play parts when communicating with others, whether in public or in private situations. He uses a number of terms to explain his ideas. The most useful of these can probably be included in one sentence: *We stage a performance through a persona.*

The idea of staging is that we do put on a show, especially in public situations. If a woman is paying for petrol at a filling station and then discovers that she has no money with her, she may well put on a performance to cover her embarrassment and to explain why she can't pay. In which case, the place and situation becomes the stage. And the stage does make a difference to the performance. For example, imagine a situation in which you are a motorist and your car won't start. If this happened at the air line in a filling station, you might mutter, but then you would look for a reason for the problem, and go back and ask for help. But if this took place in a driveway at home, then you might feel free to put on another performance involving strong language and banging of car doors to express feelings.

And again, staging can involve using the props on the stage. In the case of an interview, the interviewer can arrange props to assist in staging: an easy chair to relax the interviewee; folders in front of them to appear well informed; glasses to suggest intelligence and authority. Or, to take another example, a young man inviting a new girlfriend to his flat for a meal will tidy the place, perhaps put flowers on the table, choose some music. In fact, he will dress the stage for his performance, having regard for the needs and purposes of his communication.

The persona is the character that we adopt to play the part. Different parts in different situations require a different persona. A receptionist in a hotel would put on one kind of persona to do his job and another kind to talk to a girlfriend who takes him out for a meal.

Each persona in this case is defined by its characteristics, as one would define personality. The first one might be described as pleasant whereas the second one might be friendly. The persona is part of our way of dealing with people. It is the character out of which we communicate. In this sense it defines how we communicate. To decide (subconsciously) on using a particular persona is also to make a decision about communication style – how we talk to and use non-verbal cues with the other person.

The ability to shift from one persona to another, to choose one, is an important part of being an effective communicator. Some people believe that we have a fixed personality, or even that there is somehow something dishonest about adapting our behaviour to different situations. Not so. We need to change. It would be absurd and insensitive for someone to present the same persona for dealing with a working colleague in a production meeting and when visiting the same person in hospital after an accident.

The use of persona tends to be most obvious when one is talking about public situations, whether they involve work or leisure. If there is such a thing as a basic personality, then we would probably agree that this is the self that we present to friends and family. But still one should note that persona and performance can describe how we make contact with others in some fairly private situations. A doctor examining a patient is, in one sense, having close and personal contact with that patient. But he communicates as a particular persona in a particular way so that they both understand the 'rules' of that situation.

Or there might be the case of a visit to relatives. They may be family and it may be a private situation, but still it is possible that we would adopt a persona for dealing with, say, an aunt or uncle.

The idea of a persona is very close to the idea of role, which we will be looking at again in chapter 3. Roles exist in groups. They are about personality, behaviour and position within the group. People have roles as a member of a group – family, or friends or work group. Sometimes these roles are recognized by labels such as daughter or supervisor. A persona goes with the role. A supervisor of a group of clerical assistants would communicate in a way that they saw as being appropriate to that role. But they would also adopt a persona which fitted the role. The way that they communicated would also be affected by this persona.

A performance is the act of presenting the self. It is the act of communicating. The term is meant to suggest an intentional use of speech and NVC. The performance makes contact with the other person. A performance will probably involve some of the strategies that we have already referred to. There are some obvious and professional examples of performances. For instance, try watching a quiz show presenter on television. Watch the way that they glad-hand the game players, especially if these are members of the public. Watch the way they introduce and conclude the show. Watch the way they whip up excitement or produce laughter. This is all part of their performance. But then consider the example of parents telling off a child. This is also a performance. Watch for the way that they grab the child's attention, then enforce silence and stillness. Watch the way they hold that attention through the telling off that follows. Watch the way that this involves a mixture of disapproval, explanation and threats. Of course, the fine detail of the performance is composed of signs. Verbally, there may be phrases such as 'Don't do that!' or 'I'm not bringing you here again.' But don't miss the non-verbal aspects of the performance – gaze from beneath the brows, stiff body posture, threatening hand gestures. This is the stuff of the performance. This is how contact is made.

2.3 Communication skills

A communication skill is an ability to use means of communication effectively, with regard for the needs of those involved.

It should be emphasized that being 'effective' is not the same thing as getting one's own way. Especially where one is talking about interpersonal communication, the idea of effectiveness includes consideration for, and understanding of, the other person. It also follows that a skill involves more than mere mechanical ability to use a given means of communication. To be literate and to be able to write a letter requesting particulars of a job is one level of skill, and a useful one. It involves a degree of competence. But to be able to write a letter of application for a job that is persuasive and attractive enough to get one an interview requires deeper skills. We will refer to skills and the written form in the second half of this sub-section. More immediately, we should deal with the skills that are based on the use of spoken and non-verbal communication because face-to-face contact is the characteristic of most interpersonal communication.

Making contact with others

Making contact with others is in itself a skill. So what we have already said about strategies and self-presentation also relates to the idea of skills.

It is a skill to be able to use strategies effectively.
It is a skill to be able to present the self effectively.

Another part of making contact with others is to do with perception. This aspect of interpersonal communication is looked at in section 4 of this chapter. Perception is about observing and assessing other people while we communicate with them. But it is also a skill. We have the ability to observe people more or less carefully. We can weigh them up objectively and carefully if we want to. We can learn to do these things well and so be more effective in our communication with others. The same thing applies to looking at ourselves as communicators, and as we communicate. This is about perceiving ourselves. We can learn to do this well and be more effective when we communicate. (For examples and further discussion, refer to section 4.)

It is a skill to be able to perceive ourselves and others effectively.

From this skill another one may follow. When dealing with other people it is important to be able to 'put oneself in the other person's shoes'. This involves a sympathetic understanding of the other person's views and of their place in the situation concerned. This understanding and ability to take the view of another is called empathy. The act of doing it is called empathizing.

It is a skill to be able to empathize with others.

Another skill which is also related to the act of perceiving other people involves making a response. This response is based on how we weigh up other people, how we assess them. It is, one might say, one thing to have the skill of noticing aspects of someone else's behaviour and judging them correctly, but another thing to do something about what one has noticed. When we communicate with someone else there is a label for their reactions, which we perceive and assess. It is called feedback. We will say more about feedback in the next section. But for the moment, the important thing is to understand that the term includes not only the reactions of the other person, but also our response to those reactions. If we notice these reactions and act on them, then we are adjusting the way we communicate. We are doing something positive. Our response can take different forms. For example, if one is talking to someone about their work and the person shows signs of unhappiness, then one might respond by steering away from the subject or by trying to find out what is wrong. This all depends on exactly who is involved and on what the situation is. But, either way, one has noticed the feedback and has tried to respond to it in the best way possible under the circumstances.

It is a skill to be able to make a positive response to feedback.

One thing that helps interaction with others is if they feel that we approve of them. This doesn't mean that we have to agree with everything they say. But it does mean that they feel that basically we like them, and are prepared to give them a fair hearing. It means that we have recognized them as people. Of course all this works both ways. People like to be liked.

But once again it is a communication skill to be able to show this. If someone comes along with a personal problem – say, they have quarrelled with a friend – then there isn't going to be much communication if they feel that you aren't listening or aren't interested. Again, you don't have to approve of their quarrel in order to recognize their problem and to talk it over. And, to take another example, one isn't going to get on very well with the people one works with unless one is able to show some signs of approval towards them. To show such signs is to communicate. To do it, and do it well, is a skill.

It is a skill to be able to give signs of recognition and approval to others.

We have referred in the paragraph above to listening. Listening is also something we do when we perceive others. We don't just watch their body language and dress. We also hear their words and their paralanguage. But hearing is one thing and listening is another. Listening should mean that we are consciously aware of what the other person is saying. Too often we hear what we want to hear. We filter out the bits that we don't want to hear. We don't always give a response to what we hear, to show that we are really listening, and are actively part of the communication process. One should try to listen constructively, picking out the important bits, putting what has been said in some kind of order, trying to work out the meaning and the purpose of what the speaker has to say. Good, critical listening involves checking the logic and sense of what one is listening to, even interrupting the speaker to demand that they justify what they are saying. It involves cutting out possible distractions, from what is going on outside the window, to the colour of the speaker's trousers. It means being aware of our own prejudices, and not letting certain words or even certain topics cause us to reject what the speaker is saying, or to switch off.

All this requires an effort. It is about receiving the communication, as well as giving it. It is part of making contact with the other person. If one is not listening then there is no contact.

It is a skill to be able to listen.

Writing skills

The skills that we have referred to require the active use of the mind and the intelligence, as well as some production of verbal and non-verbal language.

We have already said that the production of this language, the ability to use such means of communication, can also be regarded as a skill. But we have already said something about what spoken and non-verbal language is, and how they can both be used to make contact with others. These two forms of communication are the basis for face-to-face contact. Yet it is also true that other means of communication, based on kinds of technology, also put people in touch with one another. We have referred to the telephone, which extends the power of speech over great distances. There is also the written word which does the same thing, though with some delay in the contact. It is worth commenting upon writing at this point, because it is another form (e.g. the letter) which is used for a great deal of ordinary everyday contact between people.

Once more, we should remember that writing is no more or less than a system of signs – marks made on a surface. The arrangement and order of the signs, which we call letters and words, depends on our learning rules. These are the rules of grammar, the conventions of this form.

The great advantage of this form of communication is that it leaves a record. It stores the message. And of course one does not need high technology to be able to make these useful marks. Once the message is stored, or encoded in the marks on the surface (probably paper nowadays), then it can be carried from place to place, kept over a period of time, be used when we want to use it, possibly again and again.

A great deal that is sensible has been said in many other books about how to write. Some of these books are referred to in the list at the back of this book. What we would stress is the notion of appropriateness, which should govern all acts of communication. Effective writing depends on your purpose and your audience, first and foremost. Some people seem to think that upper register language, elaborate turns of phrase and long sentences are a sign of good writing. Rarely is this so. We acknowledge creative writing and the private satisfaction that this brings to many people. But in fact for most people, writing, whether in their social or their working lives, is not improved by trying to be clever for the sake of it. Communication is about getting the message across in the best way possible. Usually this means 'speaking' clearly, simply and to the point.

Certainly there are various types of the written form – memos, reports, letters and the like. And they have their own conventions of presentation. These too need to be taken into account. A letter written from one company to another requesting information could be a case in point. It is a sensible convention that addresses of both companies have to be given: that provides a record of who is communicating with whom. The date provides a record of when; and so on. The 'Dear Sir' and 'Yours faithfully' phrases are part of our social conventions – like the handshake when we greet and part from someone. Providing these rules of presentation serve a purpose, they should be learnt and used in the cause of effective communication.

The trickiest aspect of writing as communication is that which is usually called style. Sometimes the word 'tone' is also used to describe the fact that we can say things in particular ways. It is sometimes suggested that we actually say the same thing in different ways. This isn't true. What we can do is put over one major message, but accompany it with a variety of minor ones. For example, if one had to write to another person apologizing for the fact that it was impossible to come to a previously arranged meeting, then the major message would be that one was not coming. But there could be a variety of additional messages: that one felt very sorry about this; that one felt completely neutral about it; that one couldn't care less; that one wanted to make up for missing the meeting in some way. All these additional messages would be expressed through style and tone.

First, the question of register might come into it. There is a difference between the upper register and formal – 'I very much regret that . . .' – and the lower register and less formal – 'I'm sorry to say that . . .'. Then there is the question of how much additional comment is thought appropriate. For example, the letter would seem more sincere and apologetic if it included a good reason for not being able to get to the meeting. Finally, there is the tricky question of the precise choice of words and phrasing. This is very much what style is about. The fact that there is a choice points to the fact that words have more than one meaning and that a particular combination of words/signs in a sentence can suggest a special meaning when taken all together. 'I hope to see you soon' is not quite the same thing as 'I look forward to seeing you soon'.

Style in writing is very much a question of voice. Read the words out loud – yours or someone else's – and describe the kind of voice that is 'speaking' them. If you have done that, and described the way that voice is speaking, then you have pretty well described the style. Which is why it is a good rule, when composing a piece of written communication, to check back its style (and accuracy) by reading it out loud. Have you said what you were trying to say? Is it right for the person who is going to read it? Have you used conventions of presentation correctly? Does it sound right when read back?

If so, then you have probably created a piece of appropriate written communication. Whether this is a school essay or a business letter, if it satisfies these criteria then it should communicate effectively. You are making contact with the other person.

Comment: shaping relationships

Interpersonal communication is most important in that it helps define our relationships with other people. It can make them or break them. It can help maintain them. And our lives are a network of relationships. The communication skills that we have already described are most influential in terms of making the contact that is to do with these relationships.

Relationships are not only to do with family, friends and lovers. We have some kind of relationship with everyone around us, not least those we work with. These relationships may not all be good ones. But even then, communication provides us with the means for a remedy. If we want to like and be liked, then we have to do something about it. Our skills in using verbal and non-verbal communication will be most important in this case. Since we cannot avoid having some kind of relationship with so many people in our everyday lives, it seems at least sensible to make these friendly and positive. We can work towards this by, for example, developing skills in giving signs of recognition and approval. We hope that others would do the same for us. When we begin to talk to another person, we begin to establish a relationship with them. It is up to us what the nature of this relationship is. But we cannot avoid this fact: communication is never simply about passing factual information, where two people are concerned. Nor is it just about having mechanical skills of communication – the practical ability to use words. It is about what we use those words for, about why and how we use them.

This is why people, even on matters of pure business, who are seeking information, say, over the phone, will start off their conversation with some enquiry about the other person's health or family. We would do well to remember that communication between people is basically about people.

Comment: situations and interpersonal communication

It is possible to categorize interpersonal communication and the situations in which it occurs in terms of oppositions. These labels are quite useful because they suggest contrast in the way that communication is used; also because they offer a quick way of looking for a range of situations through which to discuss how we make contact with others.

Formal/informal: suggests a difference between calculated and spontaneous use of communication. It suggests another contrast of public/private situations. It says something about how conscious we may or may not be of the effect of our communication on others. It would be the difference between a casual visit to the cinema with a friend and attending a première for a film where one had to talk to royalty and the famous.

Public/private: suggests a difference of context, where the communication takes place. This in turn suggests a difference of presentation and an awareness that others may be observing the communication. In public we tend to restrain our non-verbal cues, the messages about feelings. We do not say so much about ourselves. It would be the difference between discussing one's political views with the family and talking about them in a television interview.

Distant/intimate: suggests a difference of relationship between the people communicating. Also possibly a difference in the situation which they might be in. If there is distance between us and the person we are talking to, then we are inclined to be formal in the way that we use language. If the situation is intimate, then we would reveal more of our real selves, and therefore build a closer relationship with more trust. It would be the difference between discussing supply problems with the boss and discussing marriage plans with a partner.

Ritual/open: suggests a difference in the predictability of the communication used. Also possibly a difference in the familiarity with the situation of the people involved. Ritual situations often confirm relationships, attitudes and feelings of security. But they don't open up a genuine dialogue in which communication is used to explore feelings and ideas. It would be the difference between a market researcher asking someone to answer questions for a standard questionnaire and meeting someone on a blind date.

Functional/expressive: suggests a difference in the quality and purpose of the language used. The two kinds of situation make different demands on the participants. In the one case it suggests that there is a practical job to be done, in the other that the communication is needed in order to discuss and to speculate. It would be the difference between trying to buy a spare part for a car and trying to interpret the results of an experiment carried out in a laboratory.

3 REGULATION OF CONTACT

Linda's story

Hello? . . . Hello . . . Mum? Is that you? Yes, it's me. No, I'm in a coin box, so I haven't got too long. Yes, I'm fine. No, no, the training pro-gramme is going fine. That's right. Most of it is on the job stuff, so it's very practical and very useful. Yes, I'm enjoying myself. But we haven't had much spare time so far. No. I haven't seen much of Coventry . . . yes, they're moving us around from department to department, so we get a chance to see how the whole place works. . . . No, that's what I was ringing you about. We get one day's leave, and then it's on to the next store. Up to York. . . . That's right. So I shan't be coming home for a while. It really isn't worth all the travelling. I'd like a chance to settle in up there and to actually get a look at the place . . . well, I'm sorry, but the long holidays are over now. You've got to face that. I might even have my first permanent appointment in somewhere like York. And talking of holidays, I've arranged to go off with Kevin for a couple of weeks, when we do get our first break. You know his people come from up there . . . that's right. . . . No, just a minute, I'm very sorry, but I didn't know that . . . Mum, you can't have done that. You didn't even know that I was getting a proper holiday. I think it's very good of the company . . . well, I wish I was there to talk to you as well. But not to have an argument. . . . No, I'm not being unreasonable. Nor am I upsetting Dad . . . well, perhaps I should see his face now, but . . . I know it's difficult over the phone, but I'm not coming back a hundred and fifty miles to discuss some-thing which I've made up my mind about. . . . That's right. You shouldn't have made assumptions. . . . I am not being rude. Do I sound rude?! . . . Exactly. I'm standing quietly at a pay phone in a restaurant . . . what? . . . yes, by one of the assistant managers actually . . . no, I haven't . . . so, I'm sorry, but I am definitely not coming on holiday with you this year, . . . that's up to you. But do stop working yourself up about it, Mum . . . Yes, you are. I can just see your face now.

About Linda's story

This tells us how much we rely on face-to-face contact in order to convey everything we mean in our day-to-day conversations. In a literal sense, we say a great deal with our faces. And of course, other aspects of non-verbal communication also help us exchange messages with one another. It is when we are using an instrument like the telephone that we realize how important this form of communication really is. You will have noticed that Linda's mother wanted to talk to Linda face to face. Perhaps she thought that she could use her non-verbal cues to persuade Linda to change her mind about the holiday!

The point is that these signs tell us what the other person is thinking, as we say. They suggest attitudes. They influence our understanding of words used. If she could have seen Linda, her mother might have been better able to assess just how determined or sincere Linda was. And this in turn might have affected how she responded. She might have talked differently to Linda if she could have seen her as they were talking.

So these non-verbal signs convey messages which help control, or regulate, how a conversation is carried on. People in conversation use them continuously to return messages about what the other person is saying. This return of messages is called feedback.

3.1 Feedback

The idea of feedback was introduced in chapter 1 when we talked about contextualized models.

The idea of feedback has two main aspects.

One is the idea that messages are sent through verbal or non-verbal channels in response to messages from another person. The other is that these response messages are acted upon: that an adjustment of the content and style of communication may take place as a result of feedback.

This is important because it can be argued that if we are poor at giving off, recognizing or acting upon feedback, then we are that much poorer at communicating with others.

Feedback can, of course, be verbal as well as non-verbal. If a person invites someone to come round and see them, and the other person says that they can't do that, then that person has given verbal feedback.

But it is non-verbal feedback which is, if anything, more important. This is because it isn't always recognized and yet research suggests that it is the most influential channel in terms of affecting our attitudes and emotions with regard to the other person. For example, simply smiling and nodding at the other person suggests that we like them and approve of what they are saying. This feedback will encourage them to talk.

In another instance, it could be that we give negative feedback to someone else. For example, we might unconsciously clench our fists while talking to this person. This suggests tension within us, and probably some feeling of aggression towards this other person. They will get the message and either respond with a degree of aggression themselves, or perhaps just keep quiet.

This reminds us of the point that non-verbal signs are usually used unconsciously. This means that they can often be taken for a true sign of someone's feelings.

This should also remind us of the idea of strategies.

These can also be used consciously or unconsciously. And again, it is often the non-verbal signs in the strategy which are the most useful in achieving whatever it is we want to get done. For example, if we sense from their feedback that someone is losing interest in what we are saying, then we can use a strategy to try and recover that interest. If we were talking about a television programme, then we would try and make it sound more exciting. In particular, we are likely to start using more large gestures to describe action, so that the eye of the other person is drawn. We would vary the pitch and tone of our voice, so that it won't sound too boring. We would look more at the other person, stand a little closer and perhaps touch them lightly.

Our strategy would be a response to their response. And this tells us that a conversation is a continuous process of feedback of messages and adjustment of each person's approach to communicating. Once more, the rule seems to be that effective communication is, in various ways, a matter of paying attention to the other person, of considering what they need. A good communicator is observant and sympathetic.

This can apply to many of life's situations and experiences. If a child is learning to tie his or her shoe-laces for the first time, then approving pats and saying 'Well done' will encourage the child to stick at it.

If, at the end of the conversation, a girl is looking for an invitation from a man to go out somewhere, then her smiles, listening head on one side and joining in the conversation are likely to encourage him to ask her out.

If a supervisor is trying to get her clerical team to put in an extra half-hour in order to clear a job before the weekend, then she is likely to get them to do this by saying complimentary things about their work, reinforced with smiles and nods, and other signs of interest in what they are doing.

Feedback regulates our contact with others.

It helps decide how well a conversation will go.

It is our reaction to other people's communication, and their reaction to ours.

Comment

It is possible to summarize the key factors we have so far discussed in a diagram such as figure 4. Individual personal characteristics influence our perceptions, our presentation of self, our use of speech and non-verbal messages, and our reactions to others in feedback.

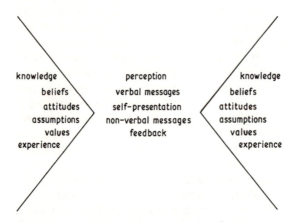

Figure 4   Interpersonal communication factors

The next section of this chapter will discuss aspects of perception: both of ourselves and of other people.

4 PERCEPTION – OF OURSELVES AND OTHERS

George's story

George Moorcroft had worked at a precision instruments factory for twenty years. He had graduated through an apprenticeship, to assembly work, to building prototypes for new instruments. He was a careful man who took a justified pride in his work. There were three other men of similar age and skills who shared the same workshop with him. Between them the men had tackled many exacting tasks, from building a miniature control arm which could pick up a human hair, to making a device for measuring the effects of pressure on any piece of material.

George was a perfectionist, with a well-regulated life. He was a neat man and a creature of habit. In fact, the only unpredictable thing in his life was the time he would take to do a job. If his work was going perfectly, George would clock out at 5.30 pm on the dot. But if he was not making the progress he desired, or the projects manager was up against a deadline, then George would work all hours to finish the job.

But the management of the company also knew that George and his work-mates would not be there for ever. And they wanted to train up some younger men as replacements. However, George was not pleased when, one day, he was faced with his new trainee, Alan.

For a start he was suspicious of Alan because he hadn't been through an apprenticeship. In fact, the old apprenticeship system had gone anyway. But, worse than this, Alan had an HND qualification and he had only been with the company for two years. George seemed to forget that by the time he was Alan's age – 24 – he had completed his own apprenticeship.

But it was when George actually first saw Alan, one Monday morning, after he had been warned of Alan's arrival, that he decided the lad wouldn't do. And he went straight to Ron Dowling, the projects manager, to tell him so.

'I mean,' said George, 'you give me a chap who doesn't even turn up in proper overalls. I'll bet he can't even use a slide-rule.'

'Ah,' said Ron. 'But you can't say that yours is exactly a dirty job, George. He doesn't need overalls to do the job.'

'But you know that's not the point. It's a matter of attitude. The chap didn't even look as though he'd combed his hair this morning. What do you think I'm to make of that?'

'I don't know. You tell me.'

'I will tell you. It means he's not careful. Not going to take care with his work if he don't take care with himself. And another thing, he's a sight too familiar. Calling me George at first meeting. But anyway, it's not just that. It's the little things. He doesn't look you straight in the eye. He was lounging on the edge of a bench when I came in. And so far, he doesn't seem to be paying attention to anything I say.'

'But you left him working?'

'Oh yes. I left him with a small calibration job.'

Ron Dowling appeared to lose interest in George's problems, and turned his attention to a small metal component lying on his desk. It was a complex valve, which immediately distracted George too.

'A nice piece this. Not our work, of course. So it must be the opposition. How did you get hold of it, Ron?'

Ron Dowling looked at George without a smile.

'Alan Lovat made that, George,' he said.

About George's story

This tells us that we shouldn't judge people by appearances. But we often do. George had a view of the kind of person who should be doing the kind of job that he was. This view was based on himself and his experience. He made assumptions about Alan, what kind of person he was and what he was able to do. And all this from a few signs. From signs of untidiness he perceived Alan to be untidy in everything that he did. And in making this assessment of Alan, George was much influenced by his own view of himself.

When we talk about perception and interpersonal communication it is all about how we assess ourselves and other people: about how we do this: about why we do it: about the results of this assessment.

Perceiving is very much about communicating because it affects what we say to other people and how we say it. George perceived Alan mainly through what he heard and what he saw. All signs must come in through our senses.

But the important thing was the meaning that he made from these signs. Especially as he was wrong about Alan.

And you may have noticed that the idea of perception is very much connected with the idea of feedback, which we have just been talking about. It is feedback messages which we perceive when we are talking to other people. And so of course, it is the non-verbal signs which are extremely important to the way we perceive others, because they are also important in feedback. In each case we need to look at the signs, their meanings and their effects. But, where feedback refers to the ways in which a conversation can be regulated and adjusted, perception goes further. We perceive people before a conversation has even started. And we perceive ourselves.

4.1 Perception of self

This is rather important, because how we see ourselves very much affects how we communicate. For example, if we see ourselves as quiet, shy people, then we aren't likely to be very positive in talking to others. We won't start conversations. We would be especially poor at talking in public situations.

And yet we weren't born as quiet, shy people. There is no law of nature that says we have to be like that. We could learn to communicate in a more positive way and then perhaps get a more positive view of ourselves. And perhaps we could learn to take a more positive view of ourselves, concentrating on what we know and what we are good at, so that then we end up communicating more positively.

There are two main aspects to the way that we perceive ourselves: we have a self-image and we have self-esteem.

Self-image

This is a view of ourselves as we think we are. This always contains a mixture of optimism and pessimism. We may think that we are taller than we really are. But then we will also probably think that some spot or blemish on the face is larger and more noticeable than it really is. This self-image includes, therefore, a notion of our physical selves, but also refers to our personality. Of course, we do not see ourselves as others see us. Again it is probably easier to prove this in the physical sense. Have you looked at yourself in a snapshot lately, or listened to yourself on a tape-recorder? Do not despair! It can be a shock, but once you stop to think about it, what you see and hear is not bad.

This self-image is developed through our relationships with others. Other people's attitudes towards us may affect our self-image. For example, a child in a lower-stream class at school may have a rather negative self-image. This would be because the child would see other people's attitudes towards 'lower-stream children' as being rather negative.

In many ways it is the personality aspect which is more important. The kind of character which we think we have, and the kind of qualities and abilities which we think we have, must obviously affect how we get on with others. If we see ourselves as being good at a particular sport, or as knowing quite a lot about that sport, then it is likely that we will talk well when it comes up as a subject.

In very general terms, one can also talk about having a positive or a negative self-image. Those people who see their skills and qualities in a positive light are likely to be more positive about talking and listening.

We also have an **ideal self-image**. This is an image of ourselves as we would like to be, and as we would like others to see us. Some people try to make their self-image match up to this idea by behaving in certain ways. It can be a good thing to try to be a 'better person'. But it can also be a bad thing to have ideas which are impossible to achieve. Failure to match up to ideals can be destructive to the personality. Parents may expect a lot from their children at school. A child can build these expectations into their ideal self-image. But then there may be a problem if, for example, the child fails examinations.

Self-esteem

In effect we have already referred to this. Esteem is about the good or poor opinion one has of something – in this case, ourselves. Whatever picture we have of ourselves, it is esteem which affects our interpretation of that self-image. For example, we may see ourselves as being bad at passing exams and getting paper qualifications. But we don't necessarily have to have low self-esteem about this. We could shrug it off because we know that we are good at other tasks. Or we might think that it is actually a bad thing to have passed too many exams because that would suggest that we were the kind of person that we don't want to be.

Esteem is about the attitude that we have towards ourselves. By looking at ourselves more objectively, it could be argued that we could improve our self-esteem, and so improve our use of communication.

One could visualize self-image as in figure 5.

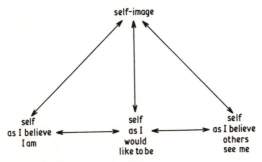

Figure 5   Elements of self-image

4.2   Perception of others

We assess other people by looking at and listening to them. This happens when we first meet others, and while we are talking with them. Our judgements are mainly about what they are thinking and feeling and are made mainly on the basis of their non-verbal cues. In this sense, perception is like a series of guesses about the other person, based on our previous knowledge and experience of them, or of people like them. We start weighing up and passing judgement on people as soon as we set eyes on them. So we cannot help perceiving others. The real question is whether or not we perceive them accurately – quite often we don't.

The longer we are with someone, the more we are likely to find out and notice them. So the better our judgements are likely to be. But in fact, many of our contacts with other people are quite brief – like interviews – so we are likely to have to make judgements on the basis of limited information. In this case, we should be careful about looking and listening, and then about making our minds up. Too often this is not the case. For example, for a while at least, we are inclined to think that because someone is wearing glasses, they must be intelligent. It may take a while to find out otherwise. And by this time we may already have acted on the mistaken impression that we have formed.

What we say to others and how we say it is significantly affected by the way we perceive them. If we see someone else as threatening and dominating, then we may try to back off, or be rather negative in what we say. And the point is that they may not see themselves like that at all. Indeed, they may not be like that – it could be that our perception is faulty because it has been careless.

So, where other people are involved we are continually monitoring their non-verbal signs in particular. From things like their tone of voice and their gaze we hope to find out what they really mean when they communicate with us. This is not just to do with what they mean by words which they may be using. It is to do with meanings about themselves and what they may be thinking, especially about us!

We perceive their personality

That is to say, we form an opinion on what kind of person we think they are. There has been much discussion about questions such as do we have a fixed personality or have we a variety of personalities? Looking back at the idea of the various persona that we present to other people, it seems that the second idea is more likely to be true. But in any case, one can agree that we usually assess others' personalities in terms of a few major concepts such as friendly or hostile, dominant or submissive. We build a picture of the person we are dealing with and, according to our view of their personality, as well as our perception of ourselves, we decide how to communicate with them.

For example, if a normally quiet and retiring person gets into conversation with someone who they perceive to be very confident and out-going, then they would probably end up doing more listening than talking.

You should also remember that there are always a variety of factors such as context, or knowledge of the subject of conversation, which should be taken into account when explaining what is happening and why.

We perceive their emotional state

That is to say, we form an opinion as to what their dominant emotions are at that time. Again, this matters because it affects how we carry on talking to them. We will decide what strategy to use. We will choose the most appropriate signs. We will use our communication skills.

And it should be remembered that it is a skill to perceive accurately what is going on. The other person might be pretending that they are calm and content, when they are not. We may notice signs like eye blinking, tensing of face muscles and slumped body posture, which suggest that all may not be well.

The other person's emotional state matters because it affects how they communicate with us, as well as how they will receive our communication. We know that. That is why we pay attention to how they are feeling. It probably isn't much good asking an employee to check a book-keeping error if you know that they have just heard that they have won the Pools!

We assess their attitude towards us

That is to say, we try to work out what the other person feels about us. We know that they will form an opinion of us, as we do of them. So we try to find out what that opinion is. That common phrase, 'It's not what you say, it's your attitude', tells us just how important attitude is in our dealings with others. Perceiving is an active, searching process, so we look for attitudes in others. We need to evaluate their position in relation to ourselves before we feel confident about talking with them. But, as with the other instances discussed, it is very possible to make mistakes. For example, signs of emotional state can easily be misread as signs of attitude. Someone who is tired and drained emotionally can easily be thought of as being negative in attitude. We should also beware of reading our own attitudes and emotions into others. For example, if we are feeling pleased and happy about something that we have achieved, then we are likely to see others as having a more friendly attitude towards us than may in fact be the case. If we show a friendly and caring attitude towards the other person and they return that attitude towards us, then there will be a good flow of communication. There will be sharing and understanding.

We make assumptions about attributes of the other person

That is to say, we make guesses about who they are, about their background and about their lifestyle. We do this from their appearance in particular. We like to be able to place other people in a role or a job. We like to be able to define them in various ways so that we can fit them into our scheme of things. So, we would guess their age from clothes, hair, face.

We would guess their job from clothes or perhaps from possessions that they have about them. Uniforms are actually meant to define peoples' jobs to others.

We would certainly want to guess the other person's sex, from things like clothes and hairstyle. Some fashions of the young, at the moment, confuse the traditional signs of sex (or gender). For example, make-up is no longer the exclusive sign of being female that it once was. This can be confusing and threatening to some people because it breaks the conventions, or rules. It also shows that the meaning of signs is not fixed.

We would try to guess someone's status. This could be in terms of the class that we suppose they belong to, or in terms of their rank within the type of job we think they do. For example, we might assign someone to a certain slot in society if they were wearing expensive clothes, or drove a Rolls-Royce car, or were addressed as 'My lord' by another person.

We would guess the other person's role in a given situation. For example, a female who appears to be between the ages of 18 and 45 and who is seen pushing a pram is likely to be placed in the role of 'mum', in the minds of onlookers. She could be the aunt of the child in the pram, she might be single and childless. But still, she will be seen as a mother.

All of this tells us that perception is not only about recognizing signs and making assessments of others. It is also about placing other people in categories. We need to define the kind of person they are so that we can decide what is the best way to communicate with them. Unfortunately, we are often too hasty in placing people in categories because we are too hasty and careless about reading the signs.

4.3 The basis of assessment

So perception is about 'reading' signs and seeking the meaning of those signs. Our judgements are based on those signs and our ability to notice them and then to make sense of them. The way we make sense of them is itself based on our previous knowledge and experience. People can become nervous in strange social situations precisely because they don't have previous knowledge and experience. They don't know 'how to behave'. That is to say, they don't know what signs to look out for and what the rules are for making sense of them. To take another situation, this is why some magazines can continue publishing successful articles on the subject of 'what to do on your first date'.

It is also important to realize that our assessment of others is based on all the information available. That is to say, our judgements are based on all the signs operating, verbal or non-verbal. Or at least they are based on a number of signs. And the information that we have could include a relationship with the other, or on things that we have already heard about the other.

Perception is a continuous process. The more we interact with another person, the more we have to go on, and so the more accurate our judgements are likely to be.

4.4 Problems with perception

Projecting our wishes onto our view of others

To some extent we see what we want to see in other people. For example, if we think that other people like us and we like them then we are inclined to think that they have the same sort of views and opinions that we have. This isn't necessarily true.

Making assumptions about others

In this case, it is as if we fill in missing information. We would assume that someone carrying a sports bag and a hockey stick is a hockey player. We assume that someone who 'looks us in the eye' is sincere. We have learnt probable meanings of signs and tend to assume that these probabilities will always be true.

Making categories of people and the signs associated with them

In one sense, it is a useful skill to be able to put labels on things. But it is dangerous to do this too quickly. Just because a man is wearing a straight white collar round his neck does not prove he is a priest, and it certainly doesn't prove that he is sweet-tempered and forgiving. The worst kind of categorizing is called stereotyping. This is when we (or the media) use a very few familiar signs to place people in jobs or roles in an uncritical and simplistic manner. And when we have placed a person in such a slot, then we assume that they have all kinds of qualities or attributes. Usually the key signs of stereotyping are those to do with appearance. For example, a bowler hat, striped trousers and rolled black umbrella is enough to categorize a man in a certain kind of job.

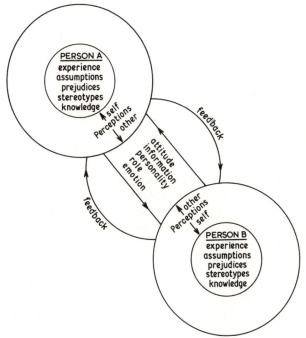

Figure 6 Process of interpersonal perception

He would also be assumed to have a certain kind of character and lifestyle.

Allowing first impressions of others to influence us

In particular we tend to pick on one or two characteristics of the other person and let these influence our opinion of that person. This is called the 'halo effect'.

For example, at a business meeting one could be unduly influenced by the fact that the other person was wearing expensive clothes and an expensive watch, and using an expensive pen. We might assume that they were rich, successful and worth listening to. That might be what they wanted us to think. So we shouldn't be too influenced by these first impressions. Nor should we jump to conclusions taken from a few details. Indeed, usually the halo effect fades away as one gets to know the other person better, gets more information about them. But we still need to beware because it isn't always possible to get to know that much about someone else.

Figure 6 illustrates key elements in the process of perception.

5 BARRIERS TO COMMUNICATION

Angela's story

Angela didn't like the early morning turn with the patients. It was hard work if you took it at the end of a long night. It was hard work if it was the first thing that faced you at the beginning of a day. It was especially hard with the old people. Many of them were so lively at six o'clock in the morning. That wasn't always a good thing.

There was old Mr Cummings in the bed at the far end. For a start, he wore a deaf aid. It was so old-fashioned that it looked like a sea shell stuck in his ear. No wonder he couldn't hear anything. Besides, she suspected he turned it down deliberately. After he had shouted 'What?' a couple of times, then Angela would lean over him to yell into his ear. That was when he came up with his favourite line, 'Give us a kiss, love'. In one week, Mr Cummings had got more kisses out of the nurses than the doctors had in two years. It was all a laugh, really. Just irritating at six o'clock in the morning. With that wonky deaf aid, you never knew if you had got through to him or not.

Of course Angela felt sorry for him as well. It was no joke having an artificial hip joint put in you at the age of 71. But then it was no joke looking after someone like Cummings. People had this idea that old

Illustration D Barriers to communication

folk grew light like sparrows. Cummings was still a big man. And it took two of them and a lot of effort to shift him around for bed changes.

When Eric Cummings opened his eyes he knew it must be six o'clock. He always woke up at that time. A habit from years of having to get up and out to beat the factory clock. The dull ache in his side was still there. He wished that he hadn't woken up. There wasn't much fun left in life nowadays. In fact there wasn't much life left. But he didn't like to think of that, even though this hip business had given him a shock.

The nurses were a starchy lot. Rather stuck-up young misses he thought. The girls in the factory had been different. Always larking around and not minding the occasional cuddle. Times had changed. He blamed it all on this women's liberation stuff. These nurses all took themselves too seriously. They wouldn't even call him by his first name. It was all Mr that, and Mrs this. He liked to feel comfortable with people. And he didn't feel comfortable here. The doctors were the worst. They would come round, look at their sheets of paper. Whisper about you with the nurses. And then when you asked what was happening, you got a mouthful of long words. Talking about . . . whatever it was . . . micturition or something like that. If they meant a Jimmy Riddle, why didn't they say so?

Anyway, it was terrible, being surrounded by all these old people. Eric sighed, jiggled his deaf aid to stop the buzzing, and tried calling for the nurse.

Angela sighed. There he was again. Probably wanted another pan or something. Her feet ached as she set off down the ward. Silly old devil, she thought. He probably didn't need her at all. Just wanted to chat. And she didn't feel like it now, especially after last night. That was the trouble with some of the old people. They didn't seem to think you were human, had a life of your own. After all, she did have a job to do.

About Angela's story

This tells us about some of the things that get in the way when we communicate with other people. If interpersonal communication is meant to be about understanding between people, then it seems that Angela and Eric Cummings didn't entirely understand one another. The problem is that there are many things that can get in the way of saying what we really want to say to others, of putting over our feelings. Because of course there is more to interpersonal communication than just exchanging messages of fact. And even the facts of his condition were not being put across clearly to Cummings by the doctors.

The factors which get in the way of free and full communication between people are generally called barriers. A more accurate word is filters, because there are rarely total barriers to understanding. You may also come across words such as 'noise' or 'interference' in some older texts on communication. It all adds up to the same idea of obstruction. And often the most important barriers are in the mind. For example, it was clear that Angela and Mr Cummings had different attitudes towards one another, coming out of their different experiences. This also meant that they had rather different beliefs and values, partly to do with their ages and partly to do with their backgrounds. We need to recognize such barriers and filters for what they are before we can do something about them. Then we may improve our communication with others.

5.1   Perception and filters

We have already discussed how poor perception filters communication (in section 4.4, 'Problems with perception'). The types of problem are also types of filter.

You should also make a link with the idea of psychological barriers because the filters are in the mind. And it is in the mind that the coding and decoding aspects of communication take place. This is where we make sense of the information about the other person that we see and hear. So we may filter before we say something or after we have heard something.

The basis of this filtering is in the assumptions that we make about other people. In one sense it is a useful skill to be able to make intelligent guesses about another person's character or behaviour.We want to know how to deal with them. But on the other hand, it isn't much of a skill if we simply jump to conclusions. It is important to learn to perceive accurately and thoughtfully. Consider the following examples. As a general instance, what about those occasions when adults talk about children in front of them, as if they are not there? Somewhere there is a filter operating which cuts out awareness of children as people and as part of the same world as the adults.

A rather more particular example of a filter could be to do with reactions to accent. It has been known for people to think that users of regional accents have less credibility and authority than those who use so-called middle-class accents. People are put through perceptual filters, and in this case the regional accent users could come off worse. At one time the BBC demonstrated the existence of this filter and the belief behind it in their reluctance to allow regional accents in newsreaders, presenters and correspondents. This is a useful example because it also suggests that the media play some part in constructing our beliefs and values. These beliefs and values in turn become filters through which we perceive the world. More of this in chapter 5.

5.2 Mechanical barriers

Communication may be blocked or filtered by physical factors in the communication process.

Noise around those talking can create a filter within the context of communication. A physical problem like deafness could block the reception of communication. A physical problem such as a lisp could impede the production of communication. Any breakdowns in equipment involved with communication would also count as mechanical barriers.

5.3 Semantic barriers

Communication may be filtered by the careless use of words. Semantics is to do with the meanings of words. If words aren't used appropriately they can't produce meanings which are likely to be understood. This comes back to the idea of codes and conventions. If we break the agreed rules of grammar or spelling or use of individual words, then we are likely to set up a semantic barrier.

'Dot cre wot yuo is ezier when fergetting' is more or less gibberish. It breaks the conventions agreed by the users of the English language code. The meaning is filtered or blocked.

Of course the meaning depends entirely on the code, its conventions and other factors such as the context within which the code is used. For example, 'drop-out' means something particular and technical to a video user or engineer. It is part of a secondary code of language to do with that technology. More generally, we use it as a piece of idiom to describe a certain kind of person.

So, another definition of this kind of barrier is useful.

Communication is blocked when we cannot attach meanings to words used because the conventions of the code are broken or because we don't know the code and its conventions in the first place. If someone talks to you in Italian, and you don't 'know' Italian, then there is a semantic barrier.

As we suggested in the first chapter, words are only signs to which meanings are attached. *Meanings exist in the mind, not in the words themselves.* So if we cannot attach a meaning to a sign, even if we know it is a sign, then there must be a barrier to communication.

5.4 Psychological barriers

Communication may be filtered or blocked by attitudes, beliefs and values. Attitudes are particular views of people, situations and events. They are based on beliefs.

These are the most common cause of difficulties with interpersonal communication. These filters shape what we say before we say it and affect how we interpret what others say to us.

Since it is inevitable that we have beliefs and opinions of some sort, some kind of selection and interpretation within the process of communication is also inevitable. But the question is how conscious are we of what we are doing to messages when we talk to other people and listen to them? We shouldn't jump to conclusions about what other people mean by what they are saying. We should think about what we are trying to say before we speak. If we don't do these things, then once more we are making assumptions. We are not perceiving ourselves and others clearly.

The effect of these barriers in the mind rather depends on who is talking to whom about what and with what intention. But obviously, these fixed assumptions that we call prejudices need to be taken seriously. And these prejudices lurk just below the surface of the mind in many of us. There has been much talk about racial prejudice in recent years. Clearly, it matters a great deal to an applicant for a job if that person is black and the interviewer has subconscious prejudices about the fact that black people are unreliable or bad time-keepers. It isn't the most blatant examples of prejudice which necessarily cause the most problems. It probably wasn't rigid male chauvinism that kept females out of newsreading jobs in broadcasting for many years. Rather, it was a kind of ill-considered prejudice which suggested to the controllers of broadcasting that this wouldn't be 'quite right'. And there was evidence that quite a few people in the audience felt the same way! More recently, there has been the case of two French owners of a British company coming to terms with national prejudice. In fact, they took on the mildly prejudiced jokes about 'Frogs' and were sensible enough not to take them as deep insults to their nationality and eating habits. They made a point of getting to know their work-force personally and built a good relationship with them. Which proves the point that effective communication can create mutual understanding and banish assumptions and prejudices.

Some books on communication refer to factors such as religion or culture as separate types of barrier. We don't, because in the end it is the beliefs and values in the minds of people involved which set up barriers when, for example, culture is a factor in a given situation. Again, the barrier is psychological. If a Sikh suffers abuse to do with his wearing a turban, or an Australian is the butt of jokes about kangaroos and beer, then it is no good blaming the turban or the kangaroo. The barrier to free and friendly communication is in the mind of the person offering the abuse or making the joke. Once more it may be seen that meanings are in the mind, not in the sign.

Comment

It is useful to visualize how these three types of barriers, or filters, affect the communication process (figure 7). Mechanical barriers in particular exist in the context and the coding processes; semantic barriers in the formulation and interpretation of the message; and psychological barriers in people's emotional processes.

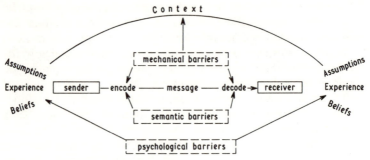

Figure 7 Barriers to communication

REVIEW

This is to help you check on the main points of this chapter, 'Interpersonal communication'.

First we said that interpersonal communication is about communication between people, usually face to face. It is about making contact with others and about how and why we do this.

1   Means of contact.
1.1   Non-verbal communication is one channel which carries messages to and from other people. It includes three codes, called body language, paralanguage and dress.
1.2   Speech is the other main channel of communication between people. It is a code, composed of signs. It includes secondary codes. The signs can be used selectively, as when we choose a register. Our verbal and non-verbal signs are special to our culture.
1.3   Contact is for exchanging messages and meanings.

2   Making contact.
This is about how we use the means of contact that we have.
2.1   We use strategies when choosing our words and non-verbal signs in order to achieve some purpose through communicating. Some strategies are used so often that they become habits, even rituals.
2.2   We present ourselves through a persona when we deal with other people. We stage a performance. We have different persona for different situations.
2.3   We can learn communication skills for getting on with other

people. For these to be effective, we must consider the other person's needs, as well as our own. Examples of skills are:

being able to use strategies effectively,

being able to present oneself effectively,

being able to perceive ourselves and others,

being able to empathize with others,

being able to respond positively to feedback,

being able to signal approval to others,

being able to listen effectively.

Skills are also to do with competence in using means of communication such as writing. Skills help create and confirm various kinds of relationships.

3   Regulation of contact.

We regulate our contact with others by giving and receiving feedback. This comes through non-verbal signs in particular.

4   Perception – of ourselves and others.

Perception is about noticing signs that tell us about ourselves and another person, and then making sense of them.

4.1   There are two main elements in the self that we perceive: the self-image and self-esteem. What we think of our self will affect how we communicate.

4.2   When we perceive others we make an assessment of them. This assessment is concerned with personality, emotional state and attitude. We also make assumptions about attributes of the other person: job, sex, status, role, age.

4.3   We base our perception on what we see and what we hear, especially on non-verbal signs.

4.4   But we perceive others imperfectly because of certain problems:

that we project our wishes onto our view of the other person,

that we categorize people too readily and too simply,

that we make assumptions too easily,

that we are inclined to be influenced by first impressions.

5   Barriers to communication.

When we communicate with others there may be factors which filter our messages when we are putting them together, or which cause us to filter the messages of others when we are making sense of them.

5.1   In the process of perception, the most common kind of filtering happens because we make inaccurate assumptions.

5.2 Mechanical barriers are to do with physical obstructions to communication.

5.3 Semantic barriers are to do with problems in conveying, receiving and agreeing about meaning.

5.4 Psychological barriers are to do with assumptions and prejudices which cause the message to be filtered. They would affect encoding when communication is given and decoding when it is received.

ACTIVITIES

1 Look at illustration D: Barriers to Communication, on page 79. List the barriers you can see illustrated in this cartoon under the headings *mechanical*, *semantic* and *psychological barriers*.

2 For the individual.
To examine non-verbal means of contact.

Construct a simple grid with the following categories: body posture, body proximity, touch, gesture, gaze.

Against each of these headings describe your use of that category of NVC in both of the following situations:

(a) To express disapproval of a middle-aged person who is 'jumping' the queue that you are in.

(b) To express approval of a five-year-old child who is showing you a drawing that he or she has done.

If possible, compare your statements about the signs likely to be used with those of someone else who has done the same exercise. See how far the grids match. Would your use of these non-verbal tactics change according to whether the person or child were male or female?

3 For a group.
To examine the use of strategies as a way of making contact with others.

Through discussion and/or role play, construct a strategy to fulfil each of the tasks described below. Describe the elements of each strategy, including verbal, paralinguistic and body language signs.

(a) To make an excuse to an acquaintance for breaking an appointment to meet him or her.

(b) To offer an argument to your boss as to why you should get an up-grading and a pay rise.

(c) To persuade a shy and reluctant person to come out with you and a group of your friends.

In each case, you may find that you need to define other factors in the situation before you can decide what is the most appropriate strategy. Feel free to define these for yourself.

If possible, compare your answer with that of another group, to see whether or not you agree on strategies, and if so how far you agree on how they should be constructed.

4 For pairs or threes.
To examine the effects of feedback, present or absent, in terms of its nature. Also how it regulates contact with others.

(a) Set up a card game with your partner. An observer would also be useful. The game must be one in which the idea is to keep the contents of your hand secret from your partner.

Now play games in two ways. One is where one person must agree to restrain all comment, expression or gesture. The other is where that person reacts freely to the tensions and fortunes of the games. After a few games, see if there is any relationship between scores and the restraint of NVC.

(b) First interview one partner, preferably not a friend, about their likes and dislikes, and their spare-time interests. In this case, work through a prepared list of questions. Do not deviate from these, or react to any of the answers. Have another person as observer.

Make an audio recording if at all possible.

Next, interview the observer as your second partner.

This time, make it a rule to react favourably and with interest to everything they say. Ask them to elaborate on points.

Again have an observer and make a recording.

Compare the two recordings and observations to see what differences there are, and in the amount of information given. Also, ask each of the interviewees how they felt about the interview. If their reactions are different, work out how and why.

5 For a group.
To evaluate the process of perception as it reveals our assessments of others.

Arrange for a stranger to come in to your group and talk for ten minutes (plus discussion) about their job.

Previously set up a grid/questionnaire for the group to fill in, commenting on your visitor. The grid sheet should be filled in after five minutes of the talk and after the discussion is over.

The grid and its terms are designed to rate the person in terms of attitude and personality, scoring these on a scale of points, all as set out in figure 8.

	6	5	4	3	2	1		
	very	fairly	not very	not very	fairly	very		
hostile								friendly
dominant								submissive
extrovert								introvert
unsympathetic								sympathetic

Figure 8   Personality assessment grid

You may add other opposed pairs to the grid.

At the end of the exercise add up points or check ticks, and compare the scores on the two sets of papers. See if there are any changes from the first to the second assessment. If there are, try to explain this in terms of what you have learnt about perception.

6   For the individual or a group.

To demonstrate the kinds of assumption that we may make about people, and how these can filter communication.

Write/note points about typical individuals in the following occupations. You may wish to include details of dress, style of speech and lifestyle.

Traffic warden   Bank manager
Vicar   Social worker
Jockey   Factory supervisor

Compare your profiles with those that other people have written to see how far they match.

If at all possible, interview real people in these occupations to see how far they match or differ from your profiles.

You will find out something about what assumptions you hold, how far they are shared with others and how valid they are.

SUGGESTED READING

Argyle, M., and Trower, P., *Person to Person*.
Patton, B., and Griffin, K., *Interpersonal Communication in Action*.
See also the resources list at the end of this book.

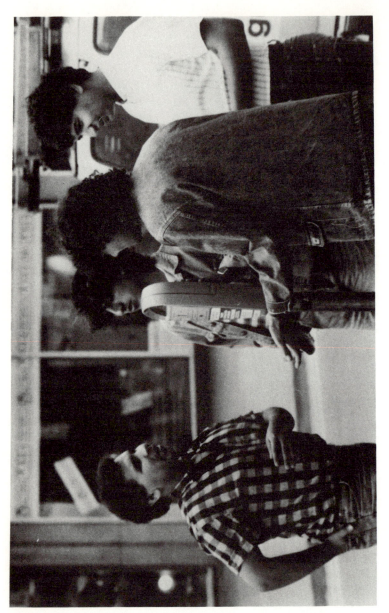

Illustration E Forming groups

·3· COMMUNICATION IN GROUPS

'A group of people is considerably more than the sum of its parts.' (Judy Gahagan, *Interpersonal and Group Behaviour*, 1975)

This chapter deals with some aspects of communication in and between groups. We provide insights into why people form and join groups and how people behave in groups. Such knowledge can help us to express ourselves more effectively in social situations.

1 WHAT IS A GROUP?

Roger's day

It's always the same, thought Roger, as he lay in bed in those flying moments between his alarm going off and his mum calling him to get into the bathroom. Once he was out of his bedroom he would not have five minutes to himself until he crept into bed again tonight.

At breakfast his dad always managed to read the paper at the same time as having multiple conversations with Mum, Gran, little sister and Roger. When Roger just wanted to sit quietly to eat his Weetabix, toast and coffee he was expected to join in the family's review of the day's news. And news included not only what the paper and the radio put out as news, but also what each of the family was going to do or *wanted to do. Could Mum persuade Dad to get home early with the car to let her have it for going to her yoga class? Could Janet get Mum to give her the money she wanted for the new jeans she saw yesterday? Would anyone listen to Gran tell us that girls never wore jeans when she was young? How could Roger convince Mum and Dad that he was up-to-date with his homework so he could afford to spend tonight at the college disco? Would they give him the money to go? They never seemed to accept what he wanted these days.*

On the way to college it was a relief to meet up with his old friends at the bus stop. Tracy and Mick were having the same problems. Every morning was the same. Tracy had started smoking at college and since her parents found out there was a lot of hassle. At least Roger's parents were prepared to let him smoke at home if he wanted to – since they both smoked themselves they could hardly do much about it.

When their bus finally came they saw it was the same as always. Full up. Standing room only. The same people always got the same seats, but most people carefully avoided looking at each other. Just because they got the same bus didn't mean they had to talk to each other.

At college Roger, Mick and Tracy rarely saw each other. Each was taking a different course. By now, Roger had got to know some of the others on his course and he always went around with the same group. It was good fun. They always spent lunch hours playing in the Sports Hall or in the Students' Union. There were some in his class who stayed in the lab and worked most lunch hours, but you wouldn't catch Roger doing that. Besides, he didn't need to, he was doing all right. At the end of the day Dave and Derek arranged to meet Roger at The George before the disco. They'd meet some of the others there as well. 'I'm not sure I can make it,' said Roger. But he didn't let on that he wasn't sure he could make it because it depended on whether his dad would give him the money.

About Roger's day

This brief glance at Roger and the people he encounters each day is perhaps typical of a young person's day. Do you think it is? At least you may be prepared to agree that we can see our days as a series of contacts with different groups of people.

Some of these groups are reasonably stable and long-lasting – like the family. Some are no more than gatherings of individuals with no real contact – like people on a bus. We meet many people in such situations – in buses, trains, cafés – but we do not form a group with them necessarily. As individuals we share a purpose but we do not make any true contact. We don't form any relationship. At college Roger felt at ease with his group of friends who shared interests and accepted behaviours. Their group beliefs and activities (for example, playing sport at lunch times) were not the same as those of other groups.

1.1 Groups we belong to

Each of us inevitably belongs to a variety of groups.

You could list those groups you joined from your own choice, for example, a youth club or a pop group. You could also list those groups you joined without a free choice, for example, your family or your school. There are many different sorts of groups with different sorts of purposes. They cater for our different needs. These needs may be short-term (an evening party) or long-term (a club that we belong to). It is interesting to consider why we join and form our various groupings.

The word 'group' can carry many different meanings and associations. **It is helpful to describe different types of groups according to their functions and qualities.** We have just noted that some are short-lived gatherings of people and others are more permanent gatherings. Some are formal, others informal. Some are small (say five people), others are large (say, several hundred). Some are local, others international. People in a group have some interest or purpose in common which brings them together.

Although **individuals in a group share common interests**, these people may not always share all of themselves. Having agreed on some purposes, people may disagree fiercely about how these purposes should be achieved. They might disagree on how the group should be organized. Some members may want all members to be equal, but other members may prefer to have a designated leader for others to follow. When people gather together there is usually some sort of struggle for power.

Relationships and patterns of communication have to be developed for the group to function. **If there is no interaction between the individuals then a group cannot be formed.** A college or school class is a collection of individuals, it rarely becomes one group, but usually consists of several sub-groups.

Family groups

The first group which most people join is the family group.

As babies we have no choice about this since we are born into a particular situation and depend on those around us for physical and emotional support. Domestic groups, whether in the form of a traditional family, single-parent family or commune of several adults and children, serve to provide security and an environment in which people can develop and grow. A vital part of this is learning how to use the languages of human communication.

The first relationships we form are with our blood relations – a phrase that indicates the prime importance of these contacts. Our needs as growing individuals must be met by these people close to us who form our primary group.

Informal friendship groups

These provide important needs of belonging. Everyone recognizes that children develop through playing with other children and with adults. But people of all ages continue to benefit from relaxed contact with others. An atmosphere in which we can communicate ourselves freely and share with others comes from a secure friendship group.

Such groups are often called *peer groups* because the relationships of these groups are between equals. These groups are most evident amongst adolescents at a time in our lives when we especially need to be with other people we like. We are often seeking to redefine our individual identity, to seek our own concept of what we are like and what we want to become. We therefore tend to seek out others who we believe are similar to ourselves. As we change so we change our group memberships. Our family relationships often undergo strains as we experience and make these changes.

Formal organized groups

These are an element of all societies. They include school and college groups, voluntary organizations such as Brownies, Cubs, Guides, Scouts, youth club, church groups, sports clubs and work organizations.

These organizations have stated aims and some of these we are required to join by the state, for instance school groups. Membership of groups helps each of us to develop his or her individual characteristics. We also develop our relationships with other people and the society in which we live. This process of development is often called *socialization*. This term describes the progress of becoming an active participating member of the society into which we are born. Being a member of many groups is necessary to develop as a person able to relate to and communicate with other people.

The functions of an organized work group may be to produce goods, produce a service or to make some sort of profit. In addition to these functions an organized group of human beings will also inevitably fulfil other functions for its members, for example functions such as developing relationships, developing images of the self and personal identity, and enabling or preventing fulfilment of people's potential talents.

More will be said about communication in organizations in chapter 4.

1.2 The nature of groups

So far we have sought to provoke some thinking about yourself and the different sorts of groups you encounter.

The rest of this chapter will concentrate on the ways groups operate and on individual's behaviour within them. Before we go on to this, however, we wish to focus our previous comments by drawing up **a list of qualities that define what a group is**:

(a) To become a group the individual members must exist in some sort of **relationship** together. There must be some form of communication between them and the group develops some sort of cohesion in order to stay together. Not all the members of the group may like each other, and they may not always find it easy to co-operate but these tensions will not be allowed to break up the group.

(b) Group members must share **common goals, purposes or interests** and recognize these. A crowd at a bus stop shares the goal of hoping to catch a bus, but they may not interact together at all and, therefore, do not form a group.

(c) Members of a group accept a system of **common values or norms of behaviour**. Some of the groups we have mentioned earlier, such as the Scouts or some schools, indicate such norms by requiring obedience to a set of rules and the wearing of a uniform. Often, however, the pressure for group conformity is less obvious.

(d) Members of a group develop **set roles of behaviour** in a particular situation. These roles can be assigned as for example in a committee when one person is elected as chairperson, one is secretary and so on. Alternatively in a specific group one person may become the silent one, one becomes the joker, one the show-off and so on. But that same person in another group may adopt a quite different set of behaviours.

With a family group and other groups that exist over a long time these set roles may change. A lifetime may take the same person from being the baby of the family to an independent child and then an adult who takes responsibility for other members of the family.

(e) This **conformity to norms of behaviour does not mean that everyone in a group behaves in the same way**. Not all relate to each other in the same way. The stability of a group usually depends on people accepting different roles and sometimes there can be a clear identification of status in which one person is openly the leader and others are followers.

(f) Members of a group have an **identity** that may be represented through their dress and pattern of behaviour.

2   WHY DO PEOPLE JOIN GROUPS?

Margery's story

The original idea and proposed route for the east-west motorway were made in the 1930s. When Margery and Nigel bought their house in Combeville everyone advised them that there was no chance of the motorway being built. The plans were dead.

So it came as some surprise, not to say horror, to read in the Evening Gazette *that the Ministry was reviving the original plans. A six-lane motorway would be built across the field at the bottom of their garden. No one in the village believed it was necessary. Certainly there was heavy traffic in the summer, but that was preferable to a massive motorway destroying the beautiful views and landscape for miles, for ever.*

'Oh God, what can we do?' thought Margery. 'We can't just let it happen without some effort to stop it. Or at least to get the route changed.' Straight away she wrote to the Gazette. *She would organize the opposition in the village. If she rang Delia in Swinton, and Nicola, and Caroline . . . she was sure they could get a petition. What about the County Councillor, the MP, and Sir Edward at the Hall?*

If she could get all of them to a meeting maybe they could set up a protest group. Force a public inquiry. At least it would delay it all and maybe . . .

About Margery's story

Having a motorway built next to your house would upset most people. But on your own it's not possible to do much about it. This little story shows one course of action that could be taken.

By organizing a local pressure group with the aims of raising opposition to the plans and proposing alternatives, it may be possible to have the plans changed. To have any hope of success Margery must convey her feelings to everyone else in the area. She must get together a wide range of people with different backgrounds, different ideas, different resources. She must persuade them to recognize their common aim to resist the motorway and form a group. People who might not normally speak to each other or have any contact with each other might be persuaded to unite. They haven't got to like each other, they haven't got to make a long-term commitment, but they must be prepared to work together with a common aim.

2.1 Reasons for forming and joining groups

There are two main reasons for people wishing to join themselves into a group: (a) to achieve a shared goal or oppose a common threat; (b) to have a sense of belonging and security.

(a) To achieve a shared goal or resist a common threat

On your own you may not be able to wield much influence, but if you can persuade others to join you, then the influence of the group can be greater than the separate efforts of lots of individuals. There are countless examples of pressure groups formed to apply pressure on decision makers to make or change a decision in their favour. Can you think of some local and national pressure groups? They could be concerned with environmental issues or the rights of a particular section of society.

For the group to perform effectively it has to achieve the group qualities that were listed in the previous section.

What sort of uniting relationship can be built?

How will the group ensure that its supporters really do pull together?

Will everyone want the leading roles?

Will no one actually want to do the donkey work?

Can such a group work informally or does it need a stated structure, for example chairperson, secretary, treasurer, publicity representative?

A group of people which is formed to achieve a set task assumes at least one common interest in its members, but there may be many more differences between the individual members which will make their relationship and communication difficult.

In such circumstances group members normally seek a formal structure which all are required to agree to. Aims have to be agreed. Responsibilities have to be assigned. The group must present a united front.

At the heart of these issues is the need for group problem solving. An individual can weigh up the evidence, formulate alternative courses of action and then select the most desirable one. However, for a group to follow this problem-solving process is less easy.

One dominating individual may be seen to wield excessive influence or the opposite may happen and the majority, who may be looking for the easy way, dominate the discussion.

The communication skills outlined in chapter 2 – of using non-verbal communication; of careful listening; of taking note of barriers to communication – all these are needed to influence a group in coming to the appropriate universally supported view.

We have concentrated on a 'pressure group' example. But these ideas are appropriate to the workings of committees, working parties set up to perform a specific task, and indeed to a total organization or association.

People in all of these sorts of group may have only one thing in common. They would not 'naturally' join together as a result of similar backgrounds, closeness of age, or a spontaneous interest through which members of a group might just drift together without any conscious intention to do so.

(b)   To have a sense of belonging and security

In this case there may not be any particular task you wish to achieve, but you simply enjoy being part of the group. You may enjoy dressing and behaving like other people to show you identify with them. In saying this people often think of mods or punks or romantics, who are obvious groups of people who have some things in common. But the same comments could be made about company executives who adopt accepted patterns of dress and behaviour at work and in their social lives. Simply wearing a certain sort of tie or a particular badge can show group solidarity. The use of communication skills to form relationships has been noted as one of the main functions of communicating in chapter 1, section 3.1.

Many groups form accidentally, simply from people with like interests gathering together. The purposes of such groups may not be formally stated, but the members simply enjoy being together and enjoy the social contact the group provides. The image of the traditional English pub satisfies these sorts of group needs.

Many people recognize in themselves and others a desire to be 'sociable'. To be able to speak to and mix with other people they identify with. **We create our own personal identity through membership of groups.** We define ourselves by a list of 'I am . . .' statements.

We feel secure in the knowledge that we share values, attitudes and beliefs with others so that to say 'I am a punk . . . a member of CND . . . a student . . . I play football . . . I live in . . .' gives us a **feeling of security.** Even if the security of the group may seem to be in opposition to other groups that other people belong to. Such statements will lead others to react in different ways: some favourably and some unfavourably.

For each of us they can provide an important reference of what we are and how we see ourselves. As children our reference group will be primarily our family group, but as we mature we choose other groups to align ourselves with. We are prepared to give up some individual freedoms and accept some imposed norms of behaviour because such conformity gives advantages. One of the main advantages is ease of communication with like-minded members of the groups to which we belong.

The opposite of this of course is that a person who shares the norms of the Rotary Club may well not find it easy to communicate and share the norms of someone who belongs to a mod group. And vice versa. Their attitudes, values, beliefs and perceptions of each other will strongly affect how each interprets what the other says and does.

Membership of groups is very much concerned with how we perceive ourselves and other people. We assign status to various groups although there may not be universal agreement on which groups confer which status. One person wears a uniform with pride which another person 'wouldn't be seen dead in'.

Comment

In this book we are seeking to make our processes of communication more conscious. Being aware that our opinions, our attitudes and our beliefs have been learned from the reference groups to which we belong can help us to see why we hold them. We tend to join with people who confirm our existing beliefs or offer us beliefs we wish to develop. We tend to reject ideas from people who challenge our beliefs.

Labelling people with group identities can prevent communication happening. Angela's story in chapter 2 (page 78) illustrated some of the barriers that labelling and placing people into stereotypes can produce. Stereotypes often result from our perceptions, even if false and prejudiced perceptions, of group memberships and identities.

We need to be aware of what group membership does to us and to other people's perceptions of us. In the final sections of this chapter we are going to look at how people communicate in groups.

3 HOW DO PEOPLE BEHAVE IN GROUPS?

Derek's story

Derek has been working at Atlantic Double-Glazing for three years. It's a good company to work for. After being out of work for some time he was lucky to get this job, selling windows.

Sure, he got fed up with standing on doorsteps trying to persuade people to listen to him. He knew that most people just couldn't afford a few hundred pounds to replace a window. He got fed up with the monthly sales briefings when the sales manager always seemed to have some new gimmick to push. He got fed up with the wage he got and the need to sell more and more to earn the bonuses. Some of the others in the sales team seemed to manage consistently good sales, but he never did. Maybe it was his patch that was the worst.

When he began his selling career he had hopes of rising to sales manager, or even of moving over into marketing. There'd be less hassle there.

He now thought he'd never make it. He'd be an ordinary salesman for ever.

Of course, there was always his other career.

When Derek left school he really wanted to be a professional footballer. He was pretty good too. He almost got an apprenticeship with Wolves. That was what he had wanted. Secretly, his mother was pleased he didn't get it. She thought that being a professional footballer would put too many temptations in his way and was not a very secure job.

He had been playing as a semi-pro now for twelve years. He still enjoyed his football and who knows, if he'd got into the League he'd be retired off by now. In the last couple of seasons he'd been captain of the club and they'd done well in the local league too – nearly got the county cup last season. Just got beaten in the final.

The young lads in the team looked to him for a lead. Wednesday nights training and Saturday afternoons were the highlights of his week. True, he couldn't last the pace for ninety minutes like he used to, but they recognized his experience. He was the old man of the club now.

Doreen thought he ought to give up at the end of this season. She said that she and the kids never saw him. What with his evening work and his training. On Sundays he was too tired to feel like doing anything. He would have to face it soon, but he had a bit more football in him yet.

About Derek's story

As captain of the local football team Derek is given respect and lives up to his role of leader and example-setter. He is most at ease with his mates at the club, whether out on the field or in the bar. He'll miss these contacts. At work, Derek is really one of the 'also-rans'. His natural confidence and personality, the fact that a lot of people know him, have helped him to make it as a salesman. But he never really feels at home with the paperwork and the pressures of keeping his sales up.

He loves his wife and children, but he recognizes that he doesn't give them as much of his time as he ought to. He's not sure whether he's a good father or not.

3.1 Roles

We adopt roles in our lives which help us to form relationships with other people. **A role is a way of behaving which is considered to be suitable for a particular situation.** From an early age we learn to play parts according to unwritten scripts provided by parents, brothers, sisters, teachers, friends and so on. There are times of course when we prefer not to play the role which others try to assign to us.

We accept to a greater or lesser extent the goals and expected behaviour patterns of a group to which we belong. There are often tensions between individual wishes and group pressures. Hence we join and leave many groupings during our lifetime. We join or form groups to serve our needs, in return for this we may have to be prepared to sacrifice some individual freedom of action.

Illustration F   Roles we adopt

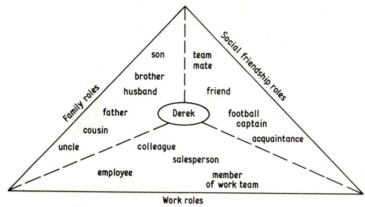

Figure 9 Types of roles in groups

It is clear from Derek's story that he plays at least three major roles in his daily life. These take place in the family, at work and at the sport/social club. Figure 9 seeks to illustrate how Derek is at the centre of a network of roles, some of which he seeks and some of which he is assigned.

As communicators it is helpful to identify the roles we play. A great deal of our education and our socialization consists of us learning what are considered to be patterns of appropriate behaviour in different situations.

The majority of our lives is spent with groups of people and we learn how to behave in those groups. If we attend an orchestral concert at a hall such as the Festival Hall in London, we are expected to sit still and quiet and listen. If we attend a pop concert at the Hammersmith Odeon in London, then we are not expected to sit still and quiet and listen in silence. If we attend a BBC Promenade Concert at the Albert Hall in London we are, by tradition, allowed to sing and dance at particular moments. If we attend an open-air pop concert then the freedom of movement, of sound, of eating and so on is again quite different. In each case we are part of an audience listening to music, but in each case we accept the role of a different sort of audience in which the patterns of behaviour are quite different.

This concept of role in communication is difficult to define, but it is useful to help explain why people behave as they do. At one extreme it may seem that if we are playing a series of roles, or merely taking on ourselves a number of dramatic characterizations, then where is the 'real me', the real person and personality within these different roles? To reconcile this apparent contradiction it is important to realize that a role is an expected pattern of behaviour, but that each person will bring to it their own personality, attitudes and experience. Within a broad framework of a role there is a lot of room for individual interpretation.

For example, if we were to compare two formal committees they would both have a chairperson and a secretary. Each of these roles is defined; however, each person that fulfils these roles will fulfil them differently. One person may be a firm authoritarian chairperson, whilst a second person may be content to let the committee discuss issues in an open way with each committee member's views being equally valued.

Another example might be to observe young children. Especially at the pre-school age from 3 to 5 years children are often trying out roles. Their play will include being mother and father, or maybe playing at being a farmer, a policeman/woman, a shopkeeper or some other occupational role which they have encountered. It is through trying these out and interpreting them for ourselves that we develop our own self-identity and our own personal approach to the roles we shall play.

In order to manage the many relationships which we enter into and to communicate with other people, we have to assume some predictability of behaviour. Hence we tend to predict that people will behave in certain ways according to categories of roles. The following list of types of roles is one which we often consciously, or less consciously use.

Professional roles

If someone is labelled a farmer, a social worker or a teacher you have certain expectations of them. You would allow a doctor or nurse to do things to you that you would only allow other people to do if they were very intimate with you. A nurse or a doctor in a hospital wears a uniform to signal their role and to decrease their human individuality and personality.

Age roles

Different sorts of behaviour are considered appropriate to particular stages of your life. You can get away with things, for example a display of tantrum, when you are a young child. A 40-year-old throwing a tantrum would be viewed differently.

Gender roles

Even though the differentiation of sexual stereotypes is rightly being challenged, there still presently remains some expectations about appropriate behaviour for men and women. If you see a man crying do you react differently from how you behave when you see a woman crying?

Look at the illustrations in this book, do they seem to support or contradict traditional gender roles?

Class roles

Again this role is changing, but in many people's perceptions, whether they are acknowledged or not, there still remain expectations about upper-, middle- or lower-class behaviour. For some people to label another person as bourgeois or working-class or aristocratic can have quite different meanings according to the perceptions and the tone of the person who says it.

Whilst these four categories of role – professional, age, gender and class – can be helpful in understanding other people's behaviour, they are not in any way fixed and we are free to choose the way we play our roles. Although we may not be able to change our gender and age we can change out of the expected behaviour patterns of a 50-year-old male. Do you have expectations of a 50-year-old male who is a solicitor from a middle-class background? What sort of person do you expect him to be? You might like to try to describe your expectation of what he looks like, the people he mixes with, the way he spends his time and the way he behaves.

Look again at the collage of photographs in illustration F: Roles we adopt. What types of roles are being depicted for this woman? Do the man and the children also seem to be fulfilling expected behaviour patterns?

These photographs reflect some traditional roles. What situations might you photograph if you wanted to challenge these role stereotypes and present alternatives?

Comment

Most books on communication that have been written in recent years include these ideas about role-playing. It is accepted as a useful way of explaining how the individual person copes with the demands made on him or her by membership of many different groups.

What we wish to stress is that we should seek to develop a range of communication styles and not become stuck in one pattern of behaviour. We accept in our written English style that what is OK for a letter to a friend is not appropriate for a report to a teacher or a manager. We also accept that how we communicate our feelings in the safety of the family group may not be appropriate for our personal expression in school or college or at work.

3.2 Norms

In a group to which we belong we may be prepared to accept the norms of behaviour which the group has developed.

These norms can be stated as formal rules such as laws in a society or rules and regulations for a school or college. Such norms are imposed quite clearly.

These norms can also be left unstated and informal. For example, in a group of people at a café it may be expected that people will be noisy, joking, fast-talking, interrupting each other, and that each person will be treated on equal easy-going terms. However, the same people transferred to their home situations may accept that at the dining table only one person talks at a time, conversation is conducted slowly, politely and quietly. Such norms are developed by the groups themselves, not externally imposed.

This development of norms usually results from the processes that have formed the group into a stable entity. It has been suggested by B. W. Tuckman and repeated by Michael Argyle that groups usually go through four clear stages in their development:

(a) **Forming** – anxiety, dependence on leader (if any), members find out about the task, rules and nature of the situation.

(b) **Rebellion** – conflict between individuals and sub-groups, rebellion against leader, resistance to rules and demands of task.

(c) **Norming** – development of stable group structure, with social norms, conflicts are resolved, cohesiveness develops.

(d) **Co-operation** – interpersonal problems are solved, the group turns to constructive solution of problem, energy is directed to the task.

The third stage of development is significant and the point at which the individual members are prepared to forego some of their own personal demands in favour of the solidarity of the group. This solidarity may be considered desirable in order to fulfil the task which the group is set or in order to fulfil the social processes of the group in supplying supporting relationships to each other.

If an outsider enters the group he or she will feel the pressure to conform to these norms. A famous study of this was carried out by an American researcher named Asch. He formed a group of people in a room who agreed to deceive outsiders who were brought into the room. The outsiders were shown several lines such as those in figure 10.

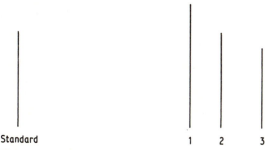

Standard   1   2   3

Figure 10 Comparisons of lines

The members of the group were told to give an obviously wrong answer about whether the standard line was the same length as line number 1, 2 or 3. The outsiders were therefore faced with a conflict between what their eyes were telling them and what they heard from a majority of those they thought were their fellow group members. Were they to believe what they thought they saw or were they to believe what they thought the other people must be seeing? The results showed that 37 per cent of the outsiders conformed to the judgement of the inner group and were thus in error. In other words quite a significant proportion of the outsiders were prepared to conform to the group pressure rather than rely on their own observation and judgement.

You might like to try a version of this experiment amongst some of your friends.

In order for it to work there must be an amount of trust amongst those taking part. The group must be prepared to keep together. Such group thinking does, of course, show that if we completely subdue our individual judgements in favour of conformity to the group this does bring dangers. George Orwell's realization of this in his novel, *1984*, in which the thought control is engineered by Newspeak, is a good example of a group dominating other people's individual perceptions and knowledge. In the fictional world of *1984* a whole international society is made to conform with an official view of the present state of the world and of recent history, which is being re-written by members of the government.

3.3 Leaders

The final aspect of behaviour in human groups which we wish to note in this section is the question of what is often called leadership. The example of Orwell's novel, *1984*, indicates a leadership principle that is totally dominating, totally controlling and totally autocratic.

There are, however, other styles of leadership. In societies that wish to perceive and portray themselves as democratic, the autocratic style, whether adopted in families, in friendship groups or in work groups, would be frowned upon. In groups with hopes of being democratic or equal, decisions are not imposed by one member.

Four major styles of group leadership are usually described as autocratic, *laissez-faire*, democratic and collective.

Autocratic

Here one person imposes his or her will on the rest. Often hostility and lack of personal commitment are the result among the other members of the group. However, in groups with formally stated hierarchies such as the uniformed services, such a style is accepted as the norm.

Laissez-faire

Here no one person or sub-group takes responsibility for decisions. In consequence little is usually achieved and there is a general state of confusion.

Democratic

Here the group welcomes initiatives from all members and no one person dominates the group. Usually there are more united common efforts and group members consider themselves to be 'we', i.e. decisions are perceived to be group decisions, shared by all. There may be an 'elected' leader or the role of leader may be rotated.

Collective

Here the group seeks to avoid the concept of a leader and operates as a team of equals. Each person is assigned equal status and power. Actions and decisions require the agreement and support of all, hence there is need for lengthy group discussion and persuasive communication skills. 'Collectives' can be slow to decide and act, but they can create a very solid and committed group.

Can you apply these broad categories of leadership to groups you know? Are you a member of an organization that seems to be autocratic or *laissez-faire* or democratic or collective?

The autocratic style is sometimes seen as being the most efficient. Decisions are often taken fast and implemented fast. The comparative loss of personal freedom and satisfaction may be accepted for the good of the group. More will be said about groups working as organizations in chapter 4.

To conclude chapter 3 we wish to explore specific examples of how communication operates in small groups.

4 COMMUNICATING IN GROUPS

Mary's story

Mary read out the letter from the solicitor. Jack Smith, who had been the youth club leader twenty years ago, had left £500 in his will for the club to spend on whatever it wanted.

As chairperson Mary had her own ideas on what the club most needed. She had also spoken to the present club leaders about their views.

But the decision about how to spend the £500 was for the youth club committee to make.

After the stunned silence and the evident pleasure at this windfall, the committee members began to air their views. Mary wanted to give them a chance to say what they each thought.

'There's only one thing we really need,' said Jo, 'and this is the chance to get it. The club is really tatty and the bar is disgusting. £500 would let us really redecorate it and install a proper bar.'

'Oh no, we've already made plans to do the decorating with weekend volunteers,' said Nick. 'This money could buy us chairs and a new TV for the lounge.'

'Yes, I agree,' said George. 'The decorating and bar building we can do ourselves. But we couldn't make furniture or build a TV set. That's what we ought to get.'

'Why do we need a new TV? We can watch telly at home. We don't come here to watch it,' argued Mandy. 'I reckon we should buy a snooker table and a table-tennis table. The ones we have now are very old.'

'Well I must say that's what I thought,' chipped in Mary.

About Mary's story

This brief extract from a meeting of a committee is intended to show how groups respond to the task of taking decisions. Each of the members has his or her own opinion of what should be done. In order for us to predict what the outcome will be we would need to know more about the present situation of the club, for example its premises, finances, membership, patterns of activity and aims.

We would also need to know more about the individual members of the committee and their status in the club, also which one of them has the ability to persuade the others that her or his view is the correct one. You may wish to remind yourself of the general aims of communication which were outlined in chapter 1, section 2. The outcome of this committee meeting revolves around effective communication in terms of assessing information, manipulating relationships between the members, persuading other people and then leading everyone to an agreed-upon decision.

The opinions of some of those members of the committee will carry more weight than the others according to their roles and status within the group and their communication abilities.

4.1   Observing group communication

We hope that from reading this chapter you now have a clear notion of how human groups exist on two levels: (a) the goal, task or purpose which brought the group of people together and (b) the social, communicating processes that enable the group to work as a group.

In Mary's story we merely indicated the words each person spoke in deciding how to spend £500. If we video-taped such a meeting we could observe a good deal of non-verbal communication, for example tone of voice, nodding of heads, facial expressions, gestures, body posture. These signs of non-verbal communication would indicate what feedback each speaker was giving and what attitudes towards the topic and towards each other the speakers wished to give, or indeed what each was giving unintentionally. Without speaking, each committee member would be likely to express a reaction to each proposal. Maybe some members were not very interested at all in what others had to say, only thinking of their own ideas.

It is possible to observe communication in groups, which is often called *group dynamics*, in two ways.

4.2   Participation and interaction patterns

We can observe the participation and interaction of people in the groups. We can see who talks most and least. We can also see who talks to whom.

Participation in a group

You can record levels of participation by drawing a circle to represent each member of the group and placing a mark in the circle for each time the person speaks.

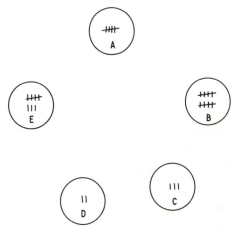

Figure 11   Participation in a group – how many times each person speaks

For example, in a group of five people, labelled A–E, we could record the participation of each person, as in figure 11. In this figure we can see that person A spoke 5 times, person B spoke 10 times, and so on.

Interaction in a group

To record the interaction between people in the group you can draw the same circles with the same labels and then indicate who talks to whom by linking the circles by lines with arrows indicating the direction of speaking. This sort of diagram is called a *sociogram*. For example, the discussion which we recorded in figure 11 might have indicated interactions such as those in figure 12.

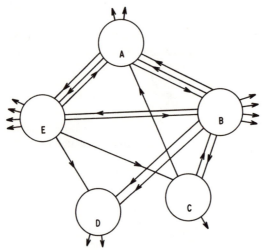

Figure 12   Interaction in a group – who speaks to whom

In figure 12 we can see that person A spoke generally to the whole group twice, spoke to person B once and to person E twice. Person B on the other hand, spoke generally to the group four times, spoke twice to person A, once to person C, once to person D and once to person E. The patterns of speaking and interaction between each of the people can thus be recorded. If one observes a group discussion and records the interactions in this way it can often be seen that the discussion can centre on one or more people with others remaining very much outside.

4.3   Group communication: tasks, relationships, individual needs

Thus by drawing circles to indicate group members we can record the levels of participation and interaction. These sorts of diagrams, however, do not really indicate what the content of these communications are. In order to do this a different method of recording the group processes is needed. We can draw up a grid as in figure 13, which records whether the group members are (a) contributing to the task of the group, and/or (b) contributing to the maintenance of the group relationships and/or (c) only concerned with their self-centred needs. By using headings for different sorts of communication, some of which are concerned with the task of the group, some of which are concerned with the members of the group contributing to the group, and some of which are more concerned with the individuals working as

Types of group communication		People				
		A	B	C	D	E
	Tasks					
1	giving information					
2	questioning/seeking information					
3	organizing ideas					
4	clarifying ideas					
5	summarizing					
6	evaluating					
7	deciding					
	Relationships					
8	encouraging					
9	harmonizing					
10	sharing/gatekeeping					
11	listening					
12	relieving tension/compromising					
	Individual needs					
13	blocking					
14	seeking attention					
15	dominating					
16	not involving					

Figure 13 Analysis grid for observing group communication according to contribution to the tasks of the group, to the maintenance of relationships in the group and to individual needs

individuals, we can build a picture of what each person is contributing to the actual discussion or meeting that is being observed.

In this analysis sheet we have not entered any details for the various people, but suggest that you use an analysis sheet like this in order to observe a group discussion. You can, of course, change the headings for the different tasks, relationships and individual behaviours. The headings that we have given provide a range of the types of contributions that people often make to group communication.

From the authors' experience of taking part in such observation exercises we can say that these methods of observing group communication often reveal that how we behave and communicate in groups is quite different from how we thought we had. I may sit in a group discussion and feel that I am making very positive contributions by giving information, summarizing, encouraging other people, listening and relieving tension. However, another observer recording an analysis of the group may have perceived my contributions quite differently. An outsider's view of my contribution may be quite different from the self-image which I have of my group behaviour. We recommend you try some of these observation exercises with groups that you know. You could, for example, have observers working with the groups following activity 1, given at the end of this chapter.

4.4   Becoming an effective group member

We spend our lives as members of various groups. In the past thirty years there have been many books published about research into group behaviour and communication. This chapter has tried to provide a brief summary of some of this research. Suggestions for further reading are at the end of this chapter and at the end of the book.

At various points in this book we use the phrase 'effective communication'. By this we mean the ability to express your ideas, to understand other people and to build satisfying relationships with other people, whether in pairs, in small groups or with larger social groupings.

This chapter has tried to provide some insight into aspects of social psychology in order to understand the communication processes that occur within groups. Membership of groups is a fundamental human need. We define ourselves, both for ourselves and for other people, by our group contacts and relationships. We often have unchallenged prejudices and stereo-types arising from our perception of people's membership of groups.

To become effective group members it is useful to take notice of the following points:

What motivates people to join groups.

The expectations of roles within groups.

The relationships between group members.

The skills of verbal and non-verbal communication.

Understanding of how groups develop from a collection of individuals to a cohesive force with their own norms of behaviour.

Understanding of group identities and the labelling of people according to group memberships and roles.

REVIEW

This is to help you check on the main points of this chapter, 'Communication in groups'.

1 What is a group?
1.1 It is a collection of people who have some shared interest or aim. We each belong to many different groups, such as :
family groups,
friendship groups,
work/organized groups.
1.2 Groups depend on relationships,
have common interests,
expect norms of behaviour,
develop set roles for members.

2 Why do people join groups?
2.1 There are two main reasons for forming groups:
to achieve a set goal,
to develop social contact and personal identity.

3 How do people behave in groups?
3.1 Each of us plays different roles according to group expect-ations and our individual personality. Roles are influenced by professions, ages, gender, class and status.
3.2 We follow group-imposed norms of behaviour.
3.3 We adopt different styles for achieving our aims.

4   Communicating in groups.

4.1   Observing group communication for achieving the task of the group and for maintaining the group relationships.

4.2   Participation and interaction patterns.

4.3   Individual functions in achieving group purposes.

4.4   Understanding ourselves and our relationships with others in the groups we belong to.

ACTIVITIES

1   For a group.
To illustrate group dynamics through a role play exercise.

Re-read Mary's story on page 109. With a group of other people enact a similar committee meeting where a decision needs to be taken about how to spend £500. Someone needs to be the chairperson to introduce and guide the discussion; someone needs to be the secretary to record the discussion; at least three other people are needed to be committee members.

2   For individuals.
To observe a formal group in action.

Go to a public meeting, e.g. town council, planning meeting, court of law. Observe the communication patterns: speaking, non-verbal communication, roles of people, how decisions are reached. You could use the charts in figures 11, 12 and 13 to record the patterns of communication.

3   For individuals.
To observe non-verbal communication in a group.

Watch a televised discussion with the sound turned off. Observe the interactions and non-verbal communication. If you have access to video-recording equipment it is worthwhile to record one of your own group discussions and to observe and analyse it later.

4   For individuals or pairs.
To analyse groups according to aims, relationships and leaders.

(a) Make a list of all the groups you belong to, beginning with the family. Why do you belong? Are they task-orientated or do they exist for social contact? What patterns of leadership do they have? What levels of conformity do they expect?

(b) Following the pattern of the diagram of Derek's roles in figure 9, prepare a similar role chart for yourself. Indicate the sorts of role you believe you adopt in family, work and social groups.

5 For a group.

To practise group interaction: to bring out concepts of role and conflict/resolution in a group.

Situation: Six passengers are trapped at Rome airport in an airliner hijacked by two men from a Middle Eastern country. Other passengers have already been released. The two men are threatening to kill passengers and blow up the aircraft. They want a quarter of a million dollars, plus a revolutionary statement printed in major western newspapers. The passengers want to get out alive at all costs. There are two government negotiators on the scene who are determined not to let the plane go or to give in to the hijackers' demands. The hijackers are jumpy and armed with dynamite, grenades and guns. The aircraft is surrounded by armed police. It is hot. There isn't enough water or food.

Characters: One passenger is a mother with a 5-year-old child. There is a middle-aged couple on holiday. One is a doctor flying to a medical convention. One is a military attaché flying to the Middle East. One is an American actress.

Players should decide on further character details before starting the simulation.

Don't forget the two hijackers and two negotiators.

Activity: Obviously the point of the simulation is to resolve the situation somehow. It should be played so that each of the three sub-groups get some time on their own to sort out their attitudes and actions. The hijackers will spend time with the passengers in order to frighten them and so put pressure on the negotiators. The passengers remain huddled in the aircraft. The negotiators may intervene now and then, but remain at a distance. They will try to argue and threaten the hijackers out of the plane. Otherwise, you decide on the details of background and activity. Give the situation time to develop. See how the passengers shape up. See how their relationship with the hijackers develops. See who gets their way in the end.

SUGGESTED READING

Sprott, W. J. H., *Human Groups*.

Gahagan, Judy, *Interpersonal and Group Behaviour*.

Myers, G. E., and Myers, M. T., *Dynamics of Human Communication*, chapter 12.

Some role play games and simulations for groups can be found in *Interplay*, published by Longman Resources Unit, 33–5 Tanner Row, York YO1 1JP.

See also the resources list at the end of the book.

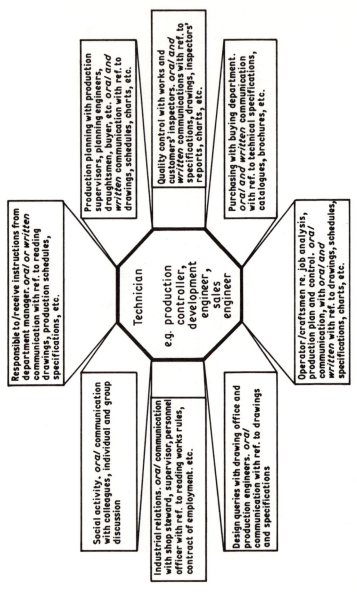

Figure 14 An employee's communication activities

·4· COMMUNICATION IN ORGANIZATIONS

'We are born in organizations, educated by organizations and most of us spend much of our lives working for organizations. We spend much of our leisure time paying, playing and praying in organizations.' (Amitai Etzioni, *Modern Organizations*, 1964)

This chapter looks at a particular sort of social group – organizations. We analyse formal and informal methods of communication used by people in organizations. Our focus is on people and their working relationships.

---

1 HOW DO ORGANIZATIONS OPERATE?

Jane's story

It had become a tradition for Mrs Taylor's class to go to a play in London at the end of the summer term. This year was to be no exception.

Jane Taylor checked with her head of department to make sure he could let her and Tom Bates out of school for a day towards the end of term. They reviewed the dates of the exams, sports day, swimming gala and parents' evenings, and the dates when other visits and field courses were arranged. As long as she avoided those dates her head of department was happy for her to take the class out.

Tom Bates, another teacher of English, had already agreed that he would go with Jane and the group.

With the approval of her head of department Jane went to see the school head to tell her that she proposed to take her class to see a play in London as she usually did each summer. The head encouraged such visits and checked her diary for any dates that must be avoided. The head gave her permission and agreed to subsidize the costs out of the school fund.

Having got the OK from the school Jane took some newspapers, magazines and brochures with details of 'What's on in London' to her next English class with her form. 'Would you like to go to London at the end of the term to visit an art gallery in the morning and see a play in the afternoon?' Jane asked. The class had been waiting for her to ask because they knew that Mrs Taylor always took her form to London.

She discussed the possible plays they might see and they agreed that they would go to the National Theatre – that had been Jane's suggestion – but they made a second choice in case they couldn't get tickets.

That afternoon Jane phoned the National Theatre to find out if they had thirty-two seats at the right price available for a matinée on one of the possible dates. She was relieved that they did have seats on the most convenient date. The people at the box office said they would hold the seats for three days till they got a cheque from her. The head had agreed to send a cheque from school.

Jane had already told the children to bring in £2 deposit by the end of the week and to pay the rest as soon as possible.

That evening after school she went to the travel agent to book the group ticket from British Rail for the time they wanted to travel. That way they had a reduced fare and reserved places on the trains. Tomorrow she would have to arrange to send a school order to the agent.

At home Jane typed out a letter for the parents of her form with details of the trip. She would have the letter photocopied ready to give to the class tomorrow.

She now had to get the money in from everyone, confirm and pay for the bookings and do some preparatory work for the gallery and the play with the class. She also had to inform all the rest of the staff. She was pleased she'd sorted it out so quickly.

About Jane's story

Organizing a group to visit London for the day is an easy task. Yet just for that Jane had to carry out several communication processes involving people inside and outside the school: speak to her colleague, negotiate with her head of department and

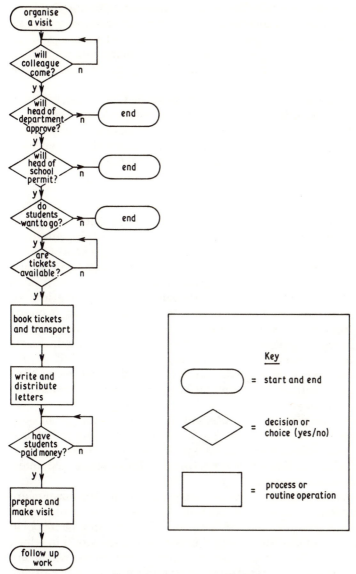

Figure 15   Flow diagram for organizing a visit

headmistress, decide the play with her pupils, phone the theatre, visit the travel agent, write a letter, complete an order form, circulate details of the visit to the rest of the school staff, send the cheque with a letter to the theatre, and so on.

Fortunately for Jane Taylor the arrangements for this visit have so far gone very smoothly. There have been no snags or opposition. Sometimes people aren't so co-operative. To take a group of people out calls for careful organization to make sure everything happens as it should. If anything is overlooked there can be problems.

It is possible to visualize the steps that Jane takes with a diagram. In order to analyse a sequence of tasks it is helpful to create a *flow chart* (sometimes called an *algorithm*) showing the series of decisions and actions that are required. Organizing a visit to London might look like the chart in figure 15.

1.1   What is an organization?

This chapter is about communicating in organizations and also about organizing for communication. The word 'organization' can refer to a particular institution such as a school, factory, office, bank; it can also refer to the process of organizing as in a phrase like 'It took a lot of organization'.

In the title of this chapter **we are using 'organization' to mean a collection of individuals who have been brought together to carry out tasks to achieve set aims**. In this sense an organization is of course a sort of group. When we discussed groups in chapter 3 we generally referred to small groups although we made some reference to formally organized groups. An organization is a group that has certain specific characteristics, as follows.

It is **deliberately established** at a certain time by an individual or group of people, e.g. it is possible to point to the date when an organization was set up – 'established in 1922'.

It develops **formally structured relationships** and interdependence between people.

It has **set objectives** which the people in the organization are seeking to achieve, for example for a business company to produce goods and services to be sold at a profit, or for a school to enable pupils to learn about themselves and the world in which they live. There may also be 'hidden' objectives which are different from the stated ones, for example in terms of health care for the whole population the medical system in the USA may be inefficient, but in terms of making profits it is highly effective.

It **divides the work to be done** between individuals and groups. There are systems and sub-systems. For example, in a national service industry some have the task of laying pipes, some installing appliances, some obtaining the equipment the organization needs, some selling the services, some dealing with accounts, some coping with taxes, insurance, staffing, safety and so on.

All the various people and their tasks require **co-ordinating into a unified effort** to accomplish the tasks and objectives.

It manages resources, both physical (equipment, materials, money) and human (work, ideas, skills). To achieve efficient and effective use of these resources is another characteristic of all organizations. For example if two people are setting up a small company to make and sell computer software, how much of their time and money must be devoted to advertising and selling their products instead of actually designing and reproducing new programs?

Finally, **effective communication between the individuals and groups** is essential if the various activities, processes and resources are to fulfil the aims of the organization. This communication takes place both within an organization and between that organization and many other organizations. For example, if the organization is a manufacturing company then it must deal with suppliers of various materials and also with many potential customers. It also has to deal with other agencies concerned with things like taxes, insurance, property and employment.

It is the purpose of this chapter to concentrate on the last of those characteristics listed above. This cannot be done without some attention to the other aspects of organizations which are listed above. However, we believe that ability to organize, whether it's an enormous multinational company or a two-person outfit, depends on effective communication between people.

At its simplest, communication as a part of organizing can be illustrated by a basic organizational task: two persons working together can lift an object which neither of them could lift on their own. But to lift that object the two people must establish a communicating relationship, agree on the objective ('Where's it got to go?'), divide the work ('I'll take this end'), co-ordinate and manage their resources ('Lift when I say go').

Our concern here is not with such small organizational groups but rather with larger-scale business organizations. We are dealing with organizations in the everyday sense of the word, meaning schools, offices, banks, churches, factories, shops and so on.

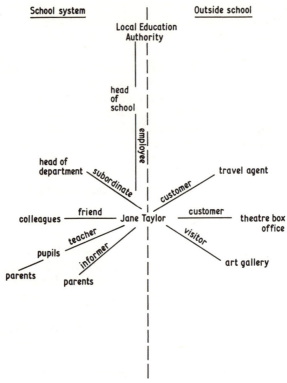

Figure 16 Network of communication relationships and roles when a teacher organizes a class visit

1.2   Relationships and structures in organizations

In Jane's story at the start of this section we saw a teacher fulfilling part of her role within the organization where she is employed. This required her to take decisions and involved her in relationships with several people. We could place Jane at the centre of a network of relationships which involves several role relationships, as indicated in figure 16.

In this figure we have placed Jane at the centre but this is obviously not an accurate picture of the structure of a whole school as an organized system of structured relationships. The traditional shape of organization structures is that of a pyramid which shows lines of authority and responsibility. A typical example applied to a school might look like figure 17.

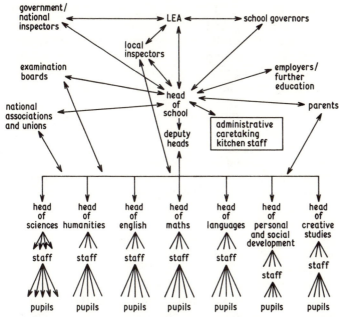

Figure 17 Hierarchical organization chart of a school showing lines of responsibility and agencies outside the school

The head of the school is given authority by his or her terms of employment to make requirements of the staff 'below'. In turn he or she is responsible to higher authorities and involved with other agencies outside the school. The local education authority (LEA) provides the majority of resources including the largest single item, salaries, for a state-maintained school (although many schools engage in their own fund-raising schemes to supplement these resources). The LEA appoints and pays the staff – a process in which governors and inspectors are usually involved alongside school staff. The governing body, a group of local politicians, interested people, parents and teachers, is ultimately responsible for the work of the school.

The head and other school staff also have regular contact with outside agencies such as examination bodies, publishers, equipment suppliers, professional associations and trade unions, parents and so on.

The staff of the school are responsible to the head but also are responsible to other senior staff who may act as intermediaries. In our story of Jane, she went to see the head to discuss her proposed visit; if the school were operated more strictly according to the hierarchy pyramid the head of department would see the head on Jane's behalf. If it were a very large school the head might decide that it is impossible and unnecessary for each teacher who wants to arrange a visit to seek her permission. The head could delegate authority to someone else to deal with such matters.

Figure 17 shows one dimension of the school organization; that is, the department structure for teaching. Do any schools you know divide the academic work up in a similar way?

Another dimension that could be used to show the structure of the same school may be not the academic work but rather the pastoral work which might be organized into 'houses' or year groups with staff responsible to a deputy head who has been given delegated authority.

To illustrate this you could draw a similar organization chart with different labels to show the lines of responsibility for the school's pastoral work.

This sort of diagram is widely used to show the formal structure of relationships in an organization. A teacher in this imaginary school might be a mathematics teacher responsible to the head of mathematics for all her teaching and also a form tutor responsible to a head of year and the deputy head for her work with the pupils in her form.

We have largely concentrated on schools so far in this chapter because we can assume that all readers have some sort of direct experience of them.

In terms of structures and networks of relationships other sorts of organizations are often represented in the same way. The divisions of work into units and sub-systems of people will obviously vary according to the size of the organization, the tasks it has to complete and its aims. A manufacturing organization will need to find ways of dealing with tasks like research and development of new and existing products; purchasing of supplies; production of goods; marketing of products; sales; distribution to customers; finance and accounting; personnel recruitment; training and welfare of staff and co-ordination and administration of all that.

As a comparison with school structures and labels, we indicate how a manufacturing/retailing company might be structured in figure 18.

Within that hierarchical structure we can focus on one department such as Marketing. To show how that department is

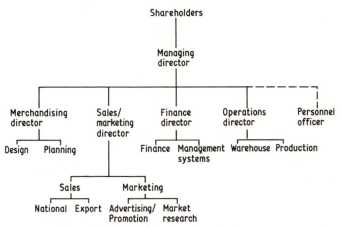

Figure 18 Hierarchical organization chart of the management of a manufacturing and retailing company

structured and how it relates to other parts of the company we shall use a spider web diagram (figure 19) which is similar to the diagram we used to show Jane Taylor's role relationships. A spider diagram focuses on the working relationships rather than the status relationships and lines of responsibility of a pyramid diagram.

There are lines of communication not only up and down in an organization, but also sideways and diagonally. People will generally speak more freely about their work and themselves and feel more able to initiate contacts with those who are perceived as being of the same status. They will be more cautious in approaching people higher in the hierarchy.

A further point to make is that there are networks of friendship and social contact that can to some extent cut across these matters of status, so that at lunchtimes, tea breaks or at gatherings like those at churches or sports clubs, people from all levels and sectors of an organization may have personal communication. A criticism of some industries has been its separation of canteen and other facilities according to status within the company. The development of group norms and loyalties which were discussed in chapter 3 is also a strong influence in these matters of open or limited communication: in some companies if you were known to be friendly with 'the Boss' people would be careful about what they told you.

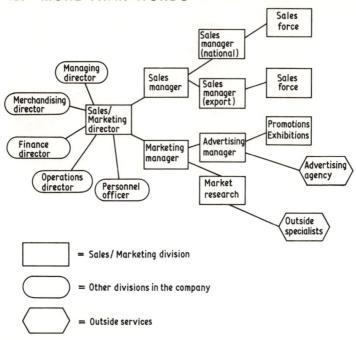

Figure 19 Spider diagram of a sales/marketing division showing lines of communication in and out of the company

Organizations develop their own norms like any other group of people. An employee who moves jobs from one organization to another within the same industry is often surprised by how different the conduct of relationships between colleagues can be.

Finally before we leave this section we must note that there are alternatives to designing organizations as hierarchical structures. One alternative is to design a co-operative structure in which all are working together with a division of labour, but without notions of superior and inferior status and power. Especially in a small organization it is possible for people to complete the necessary tasks without rigid specialization of functions – jobs can be shared or rotated, communication relationships can be open and equal.

1.3   Networks of communication

Whatever structure an organization takes networks of communication and contact will develop between the people in it. In the

spider web diagrams of the previous section we have in fact
drawn a network of communication showing the channels by
which messages flow. In the final section of chapter 3, figure 12
shows a group of five people where all channels are open; that is,
everyone can speak to everyone else.

If we keep the same number of five people (labelled A, B, C, D,
E) or imagine that these five could represent departments or units
in a larger system, we can describe other network shapes in
which not all channels are open. A network might be set up in
which one person or unit has the key position to channel or
withhold information.

There are several network shapes for a network of five in
addition to all channels open to all five.

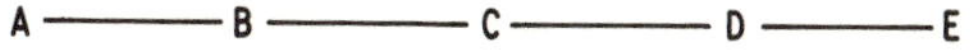

A ————— B ————— C ————— D ————— E

Figure 20   Chain network

Figure 20 illustrates a very constrained network in which C has
an important position because if a message is to be conveyed
from A or B to D or E it must go via C. If a strictly hierarchical
chain of command were the structure in an organization then the
formal network of communication would look like this. If A were
the boss he or she might occupy a position at the end of several
chains (figure 21).

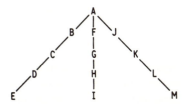

Figure 21   Chain pyramid network

Rarely does the network remain so constrained because as we
noted in the previous section some sideways and diagonal communication will take place. However, figure 21 could reflect a
managing director at Head Office (A) giving and receiving
information from regional, area and branch offices.

Figure 22   Circle network

In the circle network (figure 22), no person or unit holds the dominant position but each can only communicate with two others.

Figure 23   Wheel network

In the wheel network (figure 23), A clearly has the dominant position and is best able to co-ordinate the whole system. A's position at the centre of the network makes all the others dependent on A.

Figure 24   Y-shape network

In the Y shape (figure 24), A occupies a key position as filter and focus for communication. This shape of network could reflect the information flow between managing director (A) channelling information from shareholders (B) and board of directors (C) to company managers (D) and supervisors (E).

In outlining these possible networks of communication we have not indicated whether the flow of information is one-way or two-way. It can of course be either, depending on the situation. We suggest you try to apply these network patterns to actual situations. With a group of four other people you could experiment by sending messages orally according to different network patterns to see what effects they have on the messages and the people. If during holidays you wanted to organize yourself and four friends living in separate towns to meet for lunch one day, what network would represent the communication tasks?

Comment

Such networks of communication can be applied to many situations, not only in organizations, but also in social groupings. For example, in an extremely tense family situation it may be that some members of the family will not speak to others so that a wheel or Y network may develop with one person being the mediator. Difficult negotiations may be carried on in the same way.

Additionally such networks show that controlling the channels of communication confers power. In chapter 5 we shall consider the way in which the mass media act as gatekeepers – selecting, filtering and re-presenting the information they receive. The Y network provides a model of this process in which the editor (A) gets information from sources (B and C) and channels it to audience (D) who in turn may discuss it with groups of friends (E).

At first it might seem that the open, all-channel network is the most desirable. But for the purpose of conveying simple information it might be wasteful to have all available people discussing it with everyone else when it could simply be sent out as in the wheel.

Which networks would you use for the following tasks?
(a) A marketing director has four managers for whom she is responsible and she wishes to decide marketing strategy with them for the following year. Which network would be most appropriate? If the director is A should she use Y, chain, circle, wheel or open?
(b) The same marketing director has to decide the date of a sales conference which is held annually. Which network would be most appropriate?

There is not a single correct answer, but we suggest that in (a) the director should seek an open exchange of ideas where all of them can speak and listen to each other. If when the director called the meeting for (a) she was also in a position to decide the date for the conference she could do it there. But if when she needs to decide the date the managers are scattered around the country in their own offices she could use the wheel network: obtain from each separately the convenient dates, decide which is most convenient for all and then inform them.

1.4　Informal channels of communication

So far in this chapter we have approached the topic of communication in organizations from a rather theoretical and abstract viewpoint. In this section we are turning our attention to the ways people actually do communicate.

People in organizations may carefully lay out a plan of the structure including networks of communication. They may establish policies for keeping people informed of what is happening through regular meetings, notices or memos. They may establish policies for communication with outside agencies; for example, who is to have responsibility for signing orders and letters to go out. Most organizations do now recognize the need for such communication policies to keep people informed.

However, it is not possible to predict all the informal and personal networks and channels that develop. These informal, to some extent hidden, communication systems are a significant part of the human life of an organization. In a very restricted communication environment, such as an extreme example like a prison, this underworld of communication becomes very active. In a more open communication environment where people know that there is a systematic way of learning about things that matter from their supervisors and managers the hidden networks are less active because fear and uncertainty decrease. People have a tendency to consider that secret information is sinister information – 'Why don't they want me to know?'

The most common term to describe the unofficial, informal network of communication in an organization is *the grapevine*. This communication system based on hearsay, rumour and speculation is sometimes highly developed and fast. It is less concerned with information about how to carry out the tasks and objectives of the organization than with gossip. Gossip can perhaps be defined as information about other people, attitudes, opinions, relationships, interpretations, predictions, values. The grapevine fosters and spreads rumours and is often full of prejudice and partial truth ('Well, they say there's no smoke without a fire . . .'). Rumours spread fast especially on issues where people are uncertain or anxious. It's often said that on the grapevine the outcome of decisions is known before the decisions are taken.

The effects of the grapevine are usually seen as harmful to the smooth working of an organization, but it does not always pass on malevolent gossip. It can convey good news fast as well and may serve to boost morale through creating interest in developments and innovations.

It is generally agreed that an active grapevine is present when people are kept ill-informed through official channels of communication.

Another aspect of these informal channels is simply personal relationships between people. People have lives outside the organization in which they work. And it is natural to talk about work sometimes when you meet socially.

It's beyond the scope of this book to discuss at length the topics of industrial relations, consultation procedures or methods of employee participation in high-level decision making and formation of policies for companies. However, from a communication perspective it does seem that if people are kept well informed and involved in the issues and changes facing an organization then there is less distrust and conflict between 'us' and 'them'.

Many companies and other organizations make great efforts to keep everyone informed about what concerns them through methods such as regular newsletters or team briefings in which every supervisor at every level in an organization is required to brief the team he or she is responsible for.

1.5 Conflict

It is sometimes mistakenly thought that all problems and conflicts between individuals and groups can be resolved through effective communication. Very often the phrase 'a breakdown in communication' is used to describe the cause of conflict. This certainly does happen and misunderstandings and mistrust can develop simply because people have failed to talk to each other. Hostile attitudes can be eased by openly discussing the attitudes and their origins.

However, it must be acknowledged that conflicts do also arise because there are real differences of interest, differences of attitudes, beliefs and values. Certainly open discussion of these can enable all sides to understand and face the conflicts as problems to be solved together.

As we said in chapter 1, communication can have the purpose of changing attitudes and behaviour.

Origins of conflict can usually be placed under three headings: First, *personal* – within an individual there are conflicting ideas and desires and values; frustrations in achieving one's aims; conflicts of roles between personal inclinations and the expectations of the groups you belong to or the positions you occupy.

Second, *interpersonal* – there are differences of experience, perceptions, opinions, values and patterns of behaviour between people; there is often competition for scarce resources, whether it's for salaries, promotion, new equipment; people can fail to agree on how a relationship should be conducted in terms of status, authority or role.

Third, *in the organization itself* – potential for conflict exists when differences in status and power in a hierarchy are not mutually accepted; different parts of an organization often perceive their needs and interests in opposite ways.

Facing conflict as a problem that can be tackled is the starting point. If two people or two sides in a dispute are only interested in which one is right and which one is to blame then the conflict can only be worsened. If the sources of conflict can be defined and communicated then there's a chance that the problem can be 'managed' with both sides winning.

Ability to face conflict issues does certainly relate to communication abilities and skills in relating to and between people. An understanding of how we share meanings, how we use language and non-verbal communication, how we perceive one another and how we behave in groups can help us in our relationships. And, as we have previously suggested, the quality of personal relationships is a key factor in organizations. **A willingness to trust, to listen, to use and accept different communication styles and roles in different situations are all abilities we need for effective communication.** If you treat people with mistrust and are always on the defensive, only listen to your own ideas, always seek to use the same communication style whatever the situation, then you are likely to experience communication breakdowns.

2 CASE STUDIES AND ISSUES

Karen's story

This was the third time that Karen and Peter had worked together on the college drama society production. Audiences had been very disappointing at previous productions. Just a few students came, mums and dads and friends of the cast, and a few other local people who could be relied on to go to any serious play.

They could have done Agatha Christie or J. B. Priestley this time but neither of them felt that those two were really their scene. So it was going to be Joe Orton.

Karen thought that this time her communication studies class could work on the publicity as a class project.

She had ideas about doing more than just a few screen-print posters. But she wanted the ideas to come from the students, not from her. It was going to be their project, not hers.

The next time she met the communications class she took some of the cast with her. One or two of the class were in the drama society anyway.

'You all know that at the end of term we're putting on a play. I'd like you to take on the task of doing all the publicity. It will be useful experience for you and give you a chance to produce some real communication. I've brought Rick and Cindy in today so that they can tell you what the play's about and maybe give you some ideas of themes we can use for the posters – assuming we'll want to do some posters.'

The actors talked about the play and gradually Karen led into a brainstorming session with one of the students writing every idea up on the board. Some of them were impossible but they were all written so they could select the best ones later to develop an advertising and publicity campaign.

By the end of the session the class was divided into task groups. Each group had a job to do and had to come back with draft ideas to present to the whole class next Wednesday.

One group was drafting a letter to be sent to every student via the course tutor. They would decide later whether it was worth printing and distributing a letter to every student.

Another group was drafting a letter to send to other colleges and local secondary schools.

Another was drafting a news release to send to the local radio station and the newspapers. They were also producing an advert for the local paper. They would invite the press to see the play and a press photographer would be asked to a dress rehearsal.

Another was working with the cast to create a little presentation in costume to be performed in the shopping centre the Saturday before the performances. They thought they'd have to contact the police about that.

Another was going to rehearsals to plan a video recording of extracts to make a publicity video that would be played on a monitor in the Students' Union the week before the play.

Another was preparing ideas for posters, programmes and tickets so they would carry the same logo and theme.

Most of them were pretty keen to do it. They hadn't done anything like this before.

Karen hoped it would work. She'd have to tell her head of department what they were proposing. He might want to clear some of the ideas with the principal. Fortunately, she was usually keen to get the community into the college as much as possible.

About Karen's story

Karen had a communication problem. How to persuade people in and out of college to come to the play? The old methods of sending out posters to local schools and sticking posters around college weren't enough. Since she had done work with her class on business communication and advertising, the project fitted well.

Do you think all of the ideas are sensible? How do you think they could assess the effectiveness of the total campaign and of the particular elements within it?

This final section of chapter 4 is going to pose some communication problems and describe some particular communication issues that reflect and use the ideas in the earlier parts of this chapter. We are not usually going to offer you answers to these cases. We want you to consider possible solutions for yourself or discuss them with a group.

2.1   Channels of communication

This section takes the form of a game designed to investigate the ways in which channels of communication might operate in a *chain network*. Such a three-level chain network could be the pattern in a small hierarchy.

If you cannot get a group of people together to play the game you can probably try something similar with just three other people. Alternatively, on your own, you can try to imagine the sorts of things that could happen, but it's not so much fun if you can't actually try it out.

A model-building game

Ideally you need at least ten people and an organizer to set it up and build the original model. You need some Lego bricks or other materials with which you can make something. It could be just a complicated arrangement of paper. You need a room, preferably with tables and chairs. You need another private area that only some of the players have access to.

How to play the game

(a) Groups with at least five people in each group must be formed. We suggest that nine is the maximum number for one group. If there are fifteen people and you have sufficient model-making materials then it is advisable to form three groups of five each.

(b) Each group organizes itself into the following roles:
Builder – two or more people.
Supervisor/instructor – one or more.
Manager/planner – one or more.
Observer – one or more.

Builders will attempt to construct a model that is a duplicate of the original model built by the game organizer. Builders must not see the model until the game is over.

Supervisor/instructors take instructions from the managers to tell the builders how to construct the model. They can ask the managers questions. They act as intermediaries between the managers and the builders. Supervisors must not see the original model until the game is over.

Manager/planners go to the private area with the game organizer to look at the original model that is to be copied. The manager's task is to describe the model to the supervisors who will then tell the builders how to construct it. Managers must not let the supervisors see the model nor let the builders hear the manager's instructions.

Observers observe the whole process between managers and supervisors and between supervisors and builders. They can see the original model at the start. They must not communicate with any of the players. Observers are required to write notes about what is happening which are to be used for later discussion in debriefing after the game for all participants. The notes could include comments on things such as: How were roles allotted by the groups at the start? Did leaders emerge? Was too much or too little information given by any one? Did the managers' instructions get changed when they were passed on to the builders? What problems or conflicts arose and what were their causes? Were there frustrations, what were they and why did they arise? How could they be resolved?

The game

During the course of the game, each group has to build a model which is a duplicate of an original. This original can only be seen by managers and observers. There is a time limit set for completion of the game. This must depend on the nature of the model, but about 15–20 minutes is suggested.

Nothing must be drawn or written down except by the observers for their own use.

Only builders can take part in the construction.

The debriefing after the game

When the time is up all participants come together to discuss questions like:

How they felt about their assigned roles?

Were the channels and techniques of communication effective? If not, how could they be improved?

Did the observers' views of things differ from the players'?

Did they learn anything from the game about communicating between people?

This game has been adapted with permission from 'Communication in the organisation – a simulation', which is published in M. T. Myers and G. E. Myers, *Managing by Communication: an organizational approach* (New York, McGraw-Hill, 1982). The Laboratory Manual in the book provides many other activities, simulations, case studies and assignments related to communication in organizations.

2.2   I heard it on the grapevine

Rumours spreading on a grapevine flourish when people are hungry for information or believe that they are being kept in the dark.

Here we present a case of an office grapevine on which there is currently a strong rumour.

An office in the City

Brian presently works as a clerk in an insurance office in the City of London. He has been there for seven years and intends to stay because the people are friendly, the work is interesting – dealing with different sorts of claims – and the company give attractive fringe benefits like cheap loans and mortgages. Brian enjoys working in the City with easy access to shops, concerts, plays and art galleries. His office is a short walk from the station so he can get from home to office desk in forty minutes.

Since it's an open plan office with a relaxed but busy atmosphere there is a good deal of contact between the staff. They talk about the work but they pretty well all talk about their interests outside the office as well. Brian thought there wasn't much going on that he didn't know about.

So it came as a jolt to hear a rumour that the company was thinking about closing its City office and opening a new office in the west of England. The person who told Brian said that he'd heard it from someone upstairs who said she'd heard it from a cleaner who overheard a phone conversation one evening.

The story went round the office like wildfire. When a few of them talked about it in the pub at lunchtime there were mixed reactions. Some of them would love to get away from London to the country and if the company offered the right terms they'd jump at it. Others certainly didn't want to move and they hoped there was nothing in the story.

Arising from this situation, consider the following questions:
(a) Is there anything Brian should do after hearing this rumour?
(b) Imagine you are the office manager and you hear about the story going round the office. You have been told nothing about any such idea and it bothers you that such a story is circulating. It is certainly affecting your staff at the moment. What action (if any) would you take?
(c) Alternatively, imagine you are the office manager in this situation but you have been told confidentially that there is a proposal to move the office out of London. The decision has not been taken yet. What action (if any) would you take?

2.3 A matter of discipline?

This final case study explores interpersonal relationships, conflicts of attitudes and role expectations. There is a difference between what the organization expects and what an individual considers is his own freedom of action which he believes does not affect anyone else. It calls for an interview.

Jonathan's interviews

Jon was delighted when he left college last June to get a job as a trainee manager at the local branch of a national building society. When he began the two-year full-time National Diploma in Business Studies he had hoped that he could make a career in a bank or a building society at the end of it.

Last spring and summer when he was applying for jobs and going to some interviews he took the advice of his mum and the course tutor at college. He'd learnt about and practised interviews as part of the course. He knew that you had to play a sort of role.

So his mum bought him a plain grey suit; a nice one, though, in a modern cut. She said it would be the last item of clothing she'd buy for him because when he started a job he could buy his own clothes. He decided to have his hair cut and dyed to put it back to a mid-brown colour instead of blonde, which was growing out. For the interviews he didn't wear his earrings. He always dressed smart, never dirty or scruffy. But he thought bank managers were pretty stuffy in their ideas about clothes.

When Mr Yorke, the building society manager, appointed Jonathan he was quite impressed with the young man. He'd expected to take someone with 'A' levels, but this lad had a good reference from the college and had obtained credits in most of his course subjects. He came over well at interview. He was very presentable, smart, able to speak well, bright, keen to make a career for himself in the society and obviously able to get on with people. Mr Yorke had no doubt that Jonathan was the best applicant he'd seen that year.

None of this changed and his work was carefully done. Jonathan had fitted in well at the branch. He had come out well at the course run at the national training centre of the society. Yet last week Mr Yorke decided that he ought to speak to Jonathan about a little matter that was bothering him.

The interview went something like this.

Mr Yorke: 'Ah, come in. Sit down. I wanted to have a word with you. As you know, I'm pleased with the way you've settled in and I think you can do well in the building society. That's why I thought it was worthwhile to speak to you about a little matter that's bothering me a bit. It's not really a criticism I wanted to make. And I haven't had any comments from the rest of the staff or the customers yet. But I know you realize it's because we have constant contact with the public and customers expect certain standards.'

Jonathan: 'I'm sorry, Mr Yorke, I don't follow what you mean. I don't think I've done anything which I shouldn't have.'

Mr Yorke: 'Well, no. I've not made it clear yet. But you see, it's that thin white tie you're wearing with the pink shirt and those tight trousers with the maroon shoes. I'm not saying they're not smart. And I know you take care with your appearance. But, well, they're OK for *going out in the evening but they're not really suitable for work. Not in a job like this. I haven't mentioned it before but I've also noticed recently that your hair's become a rather reddish colour and some days you wear earrings in your ear. I'm pleased to see they're not there at the moment. Now don't get me wrong. It's not that it bothers me personally but I'm sure you can see what I mean about the customers.'*

At this point Jonathan felt he ought to say something.

About Jonathan's story

(a) We leave you to decide what you would say, in what tone of voice, if you were Jonathan. If you can work with someone else, form a pair and role play the interview from the beginning taking it on to its close.

(b) Do you think the manager is right? Could he have tackled the problem as he sees it in a different way?

(c) Do you think there are different expectations about dress and appearance for males and females at work? Are such differences justifiable?

(d) Consider a number of different organizations, such as junior schools, secondary schools, departments of colleges, offices, shops, factories, building sites and churches, in terms of their rules and conventions about dress and appearance. What sorts of differences are there? Are norms changing? In thinking about this last point try to talk to people of different ages to compare current attitudes with past attitudes.

REVIEW

This is to help you check on the main points of this chapter, 'Communication in organizations'.

1.1   How do organizations operate?
We made an overview of organizations and listed characteristics which help us to understand how they work:

they are created for a purpose,
they have structured relationships within them,
they set goals,
they divide up the work tasks,
they co-ordinate the separate parts,
they manage resources,
they communicate within themselves and with the outside environment.

1.2   Relationships and structures in organizations.
We looked at the formal and official perception of structures. These are often expressed in diagram form as pyramid- or web-shaped. Questions of hierarchy and status arise. Alternatively there can be co-operative equal status.

1.3   Networks of communication.
Information flows in several ways and networks are a way of visualizing this. An open access to and exchange of information may be desirable. Or it may be preferable, or more efficient, to restrict the flow.

1.4   Informal channels of communication.
Alongside or outside the formal structures and networks people develop their own information flows and channels for communication. The grapevine and social relationships are features of this.

1.5   Conflict.
Effective communication takes account of the differences between individuals and groups. People can learn to see the sources of their conflict. These may be
  within the individual,
  between individuals or groups,
  a result of tensions in the organization.
  If conflicts are faced they may not disappear but they can be managed as problems to be jointly solved.

2   Case studies and issues.
Finally, we focused the general account of organizational communication with three case studies based on problems and issues:
  Channels of communication.
  I heard it on the grapevine.
  A matter of discipline?

ACTIVITIES

1   For individuals, pairs or groups.
To use forms of communication to tackle set tasks.
  Re-read Karen's story on page 136. Create your own drafts of letters, posters and programmes, advertisements and news releases as described in this situation. But create them to publicize a play which you know or an alternative event with which you are familiar.

2 For individuals or pairs.

To investigate and describe structures and channels of communication.

Make a study of an organization you know, or belong to. In order to complete the following tasks you will need to interview or talk to people. Present your findings as a written report to someone outside the organization. You could also present them orally to a group. In this list of tasks we have used terms appropriate to a school. In compiling your report feel free to add further topics if you feel they are appropriate to the particular organization you are dealing with.

(a) Draw an organization chart with labels of departments and people's titles to show the total structure and the lines of responsibility.

(b) List the outside agencies that the school has contact with. This can be done under general headings rather than attempting to list every individual one.

(c) What regular meetings are held? Include those which are just for staff and pupils within the school and those which include outsiders.

(d) What systems exist for keeping people at all levels informed of what is happening? Include examples of the types of written and oral communications that are employed.

(e) What publicity brochures are produced? When and what was the most recent publicity in the local newspaper?

(f) Is there a newsletter or magazine? What is its purpose, readership, contents, style? How often does it appear? Who contributes to it?

(g) Look at three noticeboards in the school. Where are they located? Who are they aimed at? What topics are on them? Are they kept fresh and up to date? How are the notices written and designed? Do people take notice of the notices?

3 For individuals.

To develop interviewer techniques.

Arrange to interview someone who works in an organization with which you are not familiar. Topics might include means of communication that are used by the organization; how much of his/her time is spent communicating; what forms/media he/she uses; aspects of public relations, systems for keeping members or employees informed about the organization.

Prepare questions in advance, record the interview on an audio cassette, write an account of the interview to send to the interviewee. Check with the interviewee whether you have gained the facts and impressions about the person's job and the organization which he or she intended to convey to you.

4 For individuals or pairs.
To use forms of communication with appropriate conventions.

Imagine a situation at a school, college, place of work or social club which you attend. You believe that the place would benefit from installing a drinks and snacks vending machine. In the past similar suggestions have been turned down.

(a) Compose a memo to the appropriate person making a case for installing such a machine. Include why you believe it's desirable and where you would locate it.

(b) The person you wrote to has invited you to go to discuss the proposal. Prepare yourself for this interview.

(c) This person is prepared to consider the idea as a result of your suggestions but is concerned about costs and work involved in operating it. Draft a letter to be sent to vending-machine suppliers requesting the information you need. Remember to invent names and other details to make your communication authentic.

SUGGESTED READING

Evans, Desmond, W., *People and Communication*.

Myers, M. T., and Myers, G. E., *Managing by Communication: an organizational approach*.

Pearce, John, *et al. People in Touch*.

Stanton, Nicki, *What Do You Mean 'Communication'?: an introduction to communication in business*, especially part 2.

See also the resources list at the end of the book.

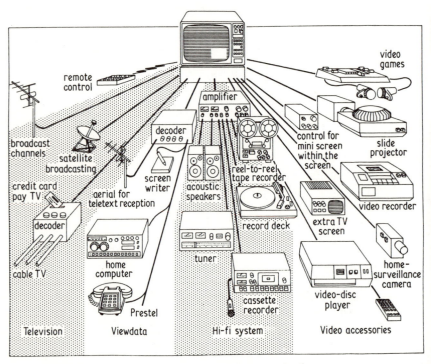

Figure 25 The TV screen and communication technologies

·5· MASS COMMUNICATION

'Television pictures tend to be unquestioned; they are accepted as being as "natural" as gas, water or electricity. They seem to be untouched by human hand.' (Stuart Hood, *On Television*, 1983)

This chapter concentrates on the mass media and takes examples from the press, radio and television. The institutions, processes and products of mass communication are the focus. The chapter considers what it is like to live in our mass media society. There is reference to mass media influence and effects. Advertising, news and visual images are discussed in particular. There is reference to current developments in communication techniques.

1 A MASS COMMUNICATION SOCIETY

Derry's story

Derry wasn't into computers. She didn't mind video games. And she did like aggravating her brother, Geoff. So the first thing she did on her Wednesday off was to take her cup of coffee into the living room and begin fooling around with the 'Caves of Orc'. Nasty creatures materialized on the screen as she penetrated deeper and deeper towards the Knowledge Stone. She had to zap them or evade them, and the shrieks of dying monsters rose to a crescendo before the door burst open, and Geoff threatened her with an even worse fate if she didn't leave the computer alone.

Derry didn't have to summon the dignity of an older sister. She was better at these games than Geoff was, and he knew it. But then, they were all the same. Electronic comics she called them. She shut down the computer and then pointedly put a video cassette in the recorder so that Geoff couldn't use the screen anyway. She munched a low calorie biscuit while watching the end of the tape that she hadn't seen yesterday. She would have to return it to Caroline today.

Derry glanced at the clock on the recorder. She must ring Caroline and Sue if they were all going to meet up in town. The other two were out of work, and would waste the whole day if Derry gave them half a chance.

Her father came past while she was on the phone in the hall and put an alarm clock on the window ledge. Derry glared at him, knowing that it was timed to go off in five minutes. It was stupid the fuss he made about her phone calls when he was picking up messages from America on that electronic mail box thing of his.

'But,' said her father, 'the company pays for it because it's worth it to them to know that I'm in touch with what's going on over there even outside working hours. They're getting overtime out of me for nothing. And I can get in touch with Philadelphia pretty well immediately. So I think . . . I don't think I have to justify myself to you. You pay your share of the telephone bills and we'll all be happy.' The alarm went off. Geoff made a face at Derry as he went out of the front door on his way to school.

Derry left soon after, with a fashionable little cap jammed on over her headphones, and the rhythms of the Cuban Swing Band dinning in her ears.

'If you took those things off, you wouldn't have to shout,' said the assistant good-naturedly, when Derry bought her copy of Heartbreak. *Derry blew him a kiss, and he blushed.*

She had a quick look at the magazine while she was on the bus. The three girls swapped magazines and tapes among themselves. Heartbreak was a favourite because of the photoplay romance stories. At one time they had taken them more seriously than they did now. But they still had a good time laughing at the wooden poses of the models, and making up new captions for the photographs.

It was like that afternoon TV programme that they watched or recorded whenever they could. It was some reject from Australia called 'Beach Babies', and it was a real cult with Derry's crowd. They all had nicknames from the series, and had a whole repertoire of 'Beach' jokes which kept everyone in fits in the pub on Friday nights.

Derry smiled to herself as she saw Caroline and Sue already waiting for her below the display screen at the bus station.

About Derry's story

This tells us something about the ways in which our lives, in work and leisure time, have come to depend on means of mass communication. The very reality of our everyday experience is partly an experience of a made-up world, invented by the media.

Derry's lifestyle and common experience is one in which she uses mass-produced communication objects, in which she can receive communication broadcast on a mass scale, in which she can communicate with others via communication systems operating on a mass scale. In other words, the telephone, television, portable tape recorders are taken for granted by her. So are the more high-tech items such as the world-wide computer link system that her father uses.

Our work and leisure experience is changing rapidly. It is the systems and products of mass communication which are the greatest part of this change.

1.1   What do we mean by mass?

We could be talking about a *system* or *product*, or *audience*. We can define mass mainly in terms of *volume, scale* and *speed*.

The system is the organization that does the communicating, such as the postal service or the radio broadcasting network. We can say that such systems are mass because they operate on a large scale and carry so many messages so widely.

The product is the object produced or carried by the system. It could be something physical like a newspaper, or something that is experienced, like a television programme. The use of the word 'product' will be discussed later on. But the point is that these products are manufactured. Whether we are talking about thousands of copies of a magazine or millions of copies of a best-selling record, the point is that we are concerned with massive numbers from a mass-production system.

The audience may also number thousands or millions. It may be composed of people who have much in common – or little except the fact that they are all listening to the same programme. But still, the numbers are sufficient that they become significant in any analysis or explanation of the communication process. They affect how and why communication takes place. This communication can be happening on a massive scale (e.g. telephone), and very fast, and in great quantities.

1.2   Mass – so what is the significance?

Mass-production of messages also means mass-repetition of messages.

The main feature of mass communication when compared with other categories, is that it does operate on such a large scale. Before we look at our media society and the operation of the media in more detail, it is worth grasping the basic fact that we need to look critically at them because they say the same sort of thing in the same sort of way so often.

And, apart from this repetition of messages, there is also the matter of penetration. Radio messages can penetrate right into the home or a car or even some remote holiday spot. Leaflets, letters and newspapers are pushed through our doors. And with these objects, and through these systems, come the ideas and beliefs which they can carry. The messages get right to us, again and again. So it should be clear that we need to look carefully at what the messages are, who is sending them, why and with what possible effect.

The sheer scale of the operation that we are describing means that it is bound to have some effect on things which everyone thinks are important – our relationships with others, what we believe in, how we describe and understand the world around us.

Mass communication is also part of that world. We suggest that there are particular aspects of our mass-communication society which are worth looking at in more detail, as follows.

1.3   Systems – availability, but no control

Our society has been greatly changed this century as systems of mass communication have become available to more and more of the population. We are more aware of what is going on in the world at large through media such as television and radio, which also use satellite and cable systems. We can keep in touch with people over great distances through a telephone network that allows us to dial direct to the other side of the world. We can buy examples of a range of technologies which can entertain us through eye and ear. There is much available to us, which can make our lives more fun, keep us in touch with others, keep us well informed about events and issues of the day. Systems are available for us to use, even if at a price which cuts out the poorer members of the population. But this view of a society playing and working with readily available mass-communication systems must also be corrected in another way.

We don't have much control of these systems, as individuals. If we don't like the way our television service is run, there isn't much we can do. If we switch off in sufficient numbers, a given programme may be dropped. But that is about all.

These remarks are intended to raise issues about the process of mass communication. The issue of whether or not the system is satisfactory as it now stands is raised when one describes the operation of the system – that is, how communication is taking place. It is our intention to raise issues as a part of communication theory, as we describe briefly these main aspects of mass communication society.

1.4   Information – a contained explosion

It is true that our society has been greatly changed by our ability to move information around very fast, over wide distances. It is the various means of mass communication that have made this possible.

Government and commerce have always depended on their ability to handle information. The sheer volume of information to be processed for an ever increasing population has encouraged the development of new technology. Local government could not manage without computer files to store their information. Banks and other businesses could not manage without cable-linked computers connecting branches with their main offices. Our holiday bookings depend on the ability of airlines and travel agents to exchange information about flights and passenger bookings via similar systems. The list of examples is endless. Our society could not be administered without mass communication.

But the population in general is also able to obtain and exchange information on a scale unequalled in the history of mankind. We now take our telephone and postal systems for granted. We are getting used to sources of information, such as the Ceefax and Oracle information services in the United Kingdom, which can be displayed on our television screens. And broadcasting and print media are themselves sources of information about many things, including other places and other peoples.

Mass communication has made all this possible. As a society, we are now used to the idea of giving, getting and using information on a mass scale.

But we should also realize that there are certain limits to this new information-biased society.

These are mainly limits of access, limits of control and limits of cost. We referred to our limited ability to control these systems in the last section. Sometimes this raises very important issues. For example, powerful institutions such as credit-control agencies or the police store information about us. In the United Kingdom data-protection legislation is being introduced, but at the time of writing there is no way of checking and changing such information, even though instances have come to light where the facts stored are wrong. And, for example, you cannot see your own medical or educational records.

The issue raised through such uses of mass communication is to do with who has the right to say what about who, who controls the system and who has access to the system.

The question of access – getting to information – also reminds us that there are other examples of limitation. These could be solved by the use of more technology. For example, it can be very time-consuming and costly to get to a main library to find out about something like building regulations. One day it may be possible to bring the information directly into your home via a cable link to the library (which stores its information in electronic files, instead of in the pages of books).

So the explosion of information via systems of mass communication affects our society deeply, but still has its limitations.

1.5 More fun – but less real choice?

We are lucky to have more time and more money to entertain ourselves than previous generations.

It is mass communication that brings us this entertainment. Entertainment has, in fact, become an industry in its own right. Our economy depends on the money spent on entertainment, in the form of things like video tapes, cassettes, television and magazines. These things are mass-produced or mass-broadcast – bought and seen in huge numbers.

Often various means of communication interact to produce examples of entertainment on a broad front. For instance, millions of people have enjoyed a science fiction film called *The Return of the Jedi*. Many have also enjoyed the book of the film, related comic books and toys, to say nothing of posters and related articles in newspapers and general magazines. They will also enjoy the video tape of the film, or watch it via broadcast or cable television. And for those who enjoyed the film, the same company offers a video game called 'Rescue on Fractalus'.

The range of entertainment is considerable. It is part of our life-style, our culture and our society. Television serials are part of everyday conversation. Girls' magazines influence the spending of millions of pounds each year on clothes, make-up and pop music.

Mass communication brings a vast range of entertainment to our society, and so changes that society.

But it is also true that the vast range does not offer the choice we may think it does. There are relatively few organizations producing the entertainment that we do enjoy. And the types of entertainment are also quite similar in many cases.

For example, one company owns three major British news-papers, *The Times*, the *Sun* and the *News of the World*. And the last two are pretty similar in look, content and treatment. Much space is devoted to pictures, sport, gossip and sex.

So this raises the issue of whether or not we get the kind of entertainment we want. It also raises the question of whether we tend to want the kind of entertainment that we get because that is all we are used to anyway.

Once more, we can support the idea of our being a mass communication society by looking at the facts. But then we also need to look at the process of communication in order to understand what kind of messages we are getting and why.

All the concepts described in chapter 1 can be used to examine, for example, a newspaper as a piece of communication. What we are now doing is adding to those ideas. It is, you may remember, basic to the study of communication that one must never take anything for granted, or believe that the way things are is a natural way of communicating.

1.6   Mass communications as extensions of ourselves

We have used the various means of mass communication in order to extend our human powers of communication.

The kind of society we have is a result of this extension. It is, most obviously, a society in which its members can keep in touch with one another in great numbers and over great distances. It is also a society in which we may scan the world via the television screen. These facts support the idea that our world has, in a sense, grown smaller. This is represented by that much quoted phrase 'a global village'. To this extent we have tackled the problem of a growing population by using machines to extend our powers of communication in face-to-face contact.

A public address system extends the scope of the human voice so that it can address an audience of hundreds. The telephone system extends the range of the human voice across continents. A magazine page stores words more accurately than human memory. A television image represents non-verbal language across great distances and to millions at a time. And now it can be argued that computers extend our abilities to think and make decisions (activities that are behind all our communication behaviour).

In our society, work activities and social activities depend, to a greater or lesser extent, on systems of mass communication. It could indeed be argued that those who do not have items such as a television and a telephone (and a computer terminal?) are socially disadvantaged. They are not fully in touch with society as a whole. And this raises further issues about what we think is essential to a healthy society in the mass-communication world that we have created.

1.7 The media and social reality

The media are part of the reality of our world.
They also help create that reality.

We are a mass-communication society because mass communication is a part of that society and its activities.

We have invented new kinds of communication to do jobs for us, in work and leisure. The driving force behind these inventions is often commercial – to make money out of communicating or to help business perform its internal communication tasks more efficiently and more cheaply. But the effects of mass communication go beyond companies and their achievement of profit.

For a start, communications businesses, including advertising, are worth so many billions of pounds, and keep so many people employed, that the economy would collapse without them.

But also the media, in particular, shape society through their ability to mass-produce messages. If we think that we are a 'modern and affluent society', for instance, then that view is partly a result of what the media show us. In this way, the media help invent our view of the world, of ourselves, of our whole society. Just as we partly base our beliefs and opinions on what friends and parents tell us, so also to some extent we base our views on what the media tell us.

To this extent, the media are, for example, part of the political process, whether they like it or not. They can show us political events as they happen. They can raise political issues. So they also help define what those events and issues are.

This in itself raises many issues about the uses and effects of mass communications. What view of the world do the media represent? How accurate is this view? How is it put together? By whom?

Once more, all of these are questions which are basic to any analysis and explanation of the process of communication.

1.8   The media – power and influence in society

The media have power and influence because of the extent of their communications operations.

We have also referred to their characteristics of repetition and penetration, which contribute to their power. It is a power to communicate on a scale unequalled in the history of mankind. The precise effects of this power and influence are not to be simply measured. This book is not designed to take on the detailed analysis and reference available elsewhere.

But the broad thrust of influence is pretty clear. We may refer back to the last section, in which we noted that the media shape our view of the world. Later we will also examine the idea that they tend to reinforce a view of the world as it is, rather than looking at alternative views.

In terms of media effects, major issues are often raised about the representation of violence or of political affairs, for example. Any general election is now largely dominated by media presentations, so far as the public is concerned. More specifically, the politician, as a media personality, has come to stand for political beliefs and attitudes. Party politics are represented through party personalities. The influence of such politicians depends, to a great extent, on the influence of the media. The precise effects of such an influence are, however, something which is much disputed. This is true, even though the notion of the power of the media is still accepted in general.

In the United Kingdom television has the power to reach 18 million viewers at peak viewing times. The most popular three UK newspapers each have the power of 3.5 million identical sets of messages, every day. And if the precise effects of such power are harder to measure than some communications analysts are prepared to admit, it still remains a quantifiable fact that, for example, television advertising does increase the sales of a given product.

If, then, there is some kind of power and influence available through the use of these media of communication, certain issues obviously appear. These may be expressed in terms of basic questions, such as who should be given control of this power? Who controls the controllers? What should the power be used for?

Conclusion

So we are indeed a mass-communication society.

This means that we use the different kinds of mass communication in various ways to conduct business and leisure in our society.

It means that the use and experience of various types of mass communication have today become a normal everyday occurrence for members of our society.

But it also means that the nature of our society has changed significantly from the experience of the last century, and it is still changing now.

Mass communication is part of our world, but is also helping to define how we see and understand that world.

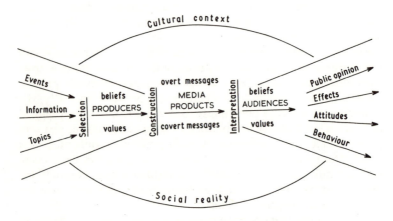

Figure 26   Model for mass media communication process

2 INTERPRETING THE MEDIA

Alex's story

Alex was aware that something was wrong as soon as he woke up. But it was nothing he could put his finger on at first. The flat looked the same. The noises of Saturday morning were the same as usual. But there was something disturbing in the air, like the first faint odour of leaking gas which alerts the senses to threat.

He made it down to the front door just as the milk was arriving. That was one custom he had approved of since arriving in England several years ago. Doorstep delivery. But he wasn't prepared for the neat-looking girl who gave him a distinctly inviting grin as she slung the bottles down. Alex adjusted his dressing gown more tightly and wondered what had happened to Whistling Charlie who usually made the delivery. He switched on the radio while he made breakfast. The news was charting the course of a trade union dispute, and Alex listened absent-mindedly while the offer made to the employers was discussed and a trade unionist was asked whether he thought they could bring management back to the negotiating table.

As Alex was leaving the building for his Saturday shopping round, he was startled to bump into a large and hairy young man wearing motor-cycle leathers. As he backed off apprehensively, noting the tattoos and heavy boots, the woman from the downstairs flat came out.

'Hallo, Alex,' she said cheerfully. 'I see you've met Don. He's our baby sitter. Reg and I came back so late last night we thought he'd better stay.'

'Pleased to meet you,' said Don, as he loomed over Alex.

Alex was pleased to get on with his shopping. He prided himself on the speed with which he could get round the supermarket, and come away with everything that he really wanted. So it was rather annoying to be held up in the checkout queue by two children in front of him. They were disputing the price of some item with the cashier. Alex noted with some surprise that they seemed to be in charge of the shopping for a whole family. But they also appeared to be well organized, and the boy won his argument when he told the cashier firmly that, old stock or not, the price on the label was what he was going to pay. Alex frowned. He felt uneasy.

He went for his usual cup of coffee, where he often met Steve and the rest of the crowd. At the table next to him a group of young men were laughing together over some magazines, and Alex leaned over to take a look while pretending not to. True Life Romance, he read on the cover of the magazines. He frowned again.

'Mandy's very good looking, but you know girls like that. They're only after one thing,' he heard one of the young men say seriously. Alex paid his bill and left.

Of course he didn't see the car, or he wouldn't have tried to cross the road in the first place. As it was he found himself lying in the gutter with a severe pain in his right leg. He lay there, very calmly considering, believing that he now knew what it was his seventh sense had been trying to warn him about. In his detachment he even found time to admire the calm efficiency of the female police inspector who had turned up to direct operations. Alex was the only person who was badly hurt. But he had caused three vehicles to crash into one another. It was bedlam. And two male passengers were crying quietly by themselves with no one taking any notice.

'Rotten men drivers!' he heard a bystander say indignantly, before he fainted.

Once in hospital, Alex found that boredom was more of a pain than his leg. The nurses were very pleasant, but they had a job to do. And under the circumstances he hadn't had time to plan for his stay in bed. For some of the day they were able to watch a communal television set, placed at one end of the ward. The trouble was that the programmes weren't much good. Alex watched bemusedly as one drama or comedy after another rolled before his eyes. The only programme he enjoyed was a comedy involving a family with a blind son who had the end of the ward in hysterics with his perceptive remarks about the rest of his family. But at night, there was nothing to amuse Alex, and he couldn't sleep, or suppress an increasing sense of anxiety.

On one particular night a friendly blond nurse named Michael turned up with a book for Alex. The trouble was that Alex had nearly got to sleep on this occasion. He peered blearily at the book's title. Alex Through the Looking Glass, he read. Panic gripped him. All was not right with the world. Alex knew that the only way to deal with his problem would be to go to sleep. Then he would be safe.

About Alex's story

You will not be surprised to hear that this story was not meant to be taken too seriously.

But it does have a serious point. Much mass media material, especially the entertainment side, tends to communicate a rather limited view of people. It repeats certain types of programme and types of people in these programmes. This is where the concepts of genre and stereotyping come in. We will say more of these a little later.

The main thing is to recognize that these limitations are there, and do mean that our view of the world is, to an extent, limited and distorted. Recognition of this problem is, in fact, a good way of correcting it. Alex's alternative experience was one in which men, women, young people, did not behave as they do in the media.

The media represents a world in which nurses are usually angels and female, and young men are rarely interested in romance and love.

You will recognize other points that the story tries to make. You will probably not agree with all of them. And certainly the media do not have the monopoly on generalizations about people and groups. We utter some of them in our everyday observations and opinions.

But then, what we say has a limited audience. This is certainly not true of the media whose messages can, we have noted, reinforce through sheer repetition.

There is more happening than meets the eye, in the process of communication through the media. We must interpret this process, to find out what is going on. We use certain terms/ concepts to do this interpreting.

2.1 Mediation

is a general term used to describe the transformation of original material (scripts, events, etc.) when it is processed through any one of the mass media.

Any form of communication is only a set of signs standing in place of some original event, object, idea, etc., and so a kind of mediation must always take place when communication takes place. A film showing tigers in the wild is only showing tigers. It is not bringing us the real tigers or the original experience.

But the term mediation is usually taken to mean more than just 'standing in place of' and so transforming. We use it with reference to the media because they often actively transform all that they represent.

Again, it is convenient to leave out fiction material in any discussion. It is obvious that fiction does not pretend to present factual experience. Such material may mediate the author's intentions. Or again, one could look at the way in which a television version of a novel like *Mansfield Park* mediates that original novel. But in any case, we are pretty sure that a transformation has taken place.

However, much media is factual, or purports to be so. It is here that we should look most carefully at the idea of mediation.

This idea should cause us to ask what kind of change has taken place from the original to the media version. And how that change has taken place, why and with what effect. All the points that follow in this second section of the chapter build on the concept of mediation, and confirm the fact that it really does matter that it happens.

For example, sport is mediated in the way that television represents its various events. On a mechanical level, football matches are repackaged by the editing process: they have the illusion of being seen as they happen, but time is compressed until only the drama and the goals remain.

Even when a match is shown live, the football is very much a mediated event. The viewer becomes a god through the mediating power of the camera which can survey the entire pitch from above, or the details of play as if we are out there on the pitch. Video discs permit the mediators to control time, giving us an instant flashback of action replay on the goals scored. And the commentator is actually heard as mediator, producing explanations and interpretations of events on the field which might never have occurred to us if we had been at the match itself.

For example, the events and the very clothes of the fashion world are mediated through magazines. In this instance, we note two things: that different media can work together in the mediation process – creating a notion of what is fashionable at any point; and that there can be creation as well as transformation in the mediation process. The idea of what is fashionable for summer wear, for instance, is not just the result of articles on fashion shows or what is available in certain shops, but also of opinions coming from the people who write the articles and take the pictures. At the time of writing, the 'V-back' look is fashionable in a wide range of women's clothes. The magazines are not just mediating what is 'out there'. The fashion articles become a source of information and ideas in themselves.

In this way the media can be an active part of our cultural life. Mediation is an active process.

In this way the media help create culture, as well as our social reality.

2.2   Selection and construction

The content of any programme or newspaper is the result of a process of selection and construction.

Any example of media material is an example of a piece of communication that has been produced from a number of possible sources, and put together from only some of these. What is more, it has been put together in a certain way. What has been left out may be as important as what has been put in.

The way the material has been constructed will depend on a number of assumptions made by the media makers – assumptions, working practices, habits, conventions, to do with the 'normal' or 'proper' way to handle a given subject or a given type of programme, article, etc.

In this book we tend, by choice, to look at examples from television and newspapers. But the terms used, and the ideas they contain, could be used in any one of the media.

For example, a pop single is constructed from a number of tracks laid down in the studio. Some of these are selected from different takes and put together (mixed) to create a number that never existed in this form in the first place. And indeed, there may be several numbers which could have been chosen for this single release. Only one is chosen. The studio (and a record company) have selected and constructed this piece of communication because they think it will entertain a mass audience and will sell.

For example, a typical radio news-magazine programme is constructed from many pieces of material available – tapes, live voice, cable links with foreign places. And all these pieces of material may be on a variety of subjects, treated in a variety of ways. In the end, the programme editor will preside over a selection process which leaves out some material, reworks other pieces, sets up a running order and a time for each item. He has made decisions about that piece of communication which we call the programme.

We notice that, in the category of the media especially, it is very obvious that communication is not a 'natural' process. It is an activity that is performed in certain ways for certain reasons. In the end, the media are usually trying to chase audience figures and profits. The ways in which they communicate become more understandable when one remembers these two basic facts.

We may also notice that the media are distinctive in that items of media communication are produced by a group of people, working collaboratively, rather than by individuals. The idea of an individual creator is attractive to us because our culture leads us to believe in individualism – personalities, stars. But the facts are different.

For example, this book is the result of collaboration between two authors, an editor, a secretary, photographers and artists, printers and others. It is constructed by a number of people. It didn't just happen. You are reading these words because we decided that we wanted to communicate about communicating.

2.3   Product

The term 'product' draws attention to the fact that the media manufacture 'goods' which are bought by the audience as 'consumers'.

The term is used to draw attention to the fact that most pieces of communication coming through the media have to be promoted and sold in a marketplace.

Methuen is not producing this book only because it believes it can be useful. The company also believes that it will make money and enable them to produce more books.

The concept of product includes the ideas that the communication is produced in quantity and is sold. It is useful to an understanding of how and why communication takes place because often these facts are obscured.

For example, television series are made on a production line called a studio, just like a make of car. They will be sold through publicity work, trailers on television, possibly newspaper ads, just like the car. The television company is also trying to please its consumers, called the audience. (Even the BBC must chase the ratings and compete, in order to justify its licence fee.) The consumers in this country also pay for the product, through this licence fee, or through that proportion of the price of other products which is set aside by advertisers to pay for advertising. To say all this is neither to praise nor to condemn the end result. It simply illustrates the how and why of the communication process. And perhaps it will stop some people from pretending that there is either art or commerce in mass communication, when often the truth lies somewhere between these two ideas.

2.4   Ownership and finance

Media messages come from somewhere, and must be paid for by someone.

We can interpret the media and the way they communicate with more understanding if we understand their sources – of ownership as well as finance. It is clear that the cost element, as well as the ability to own all this message-making technology, distinguishes a film, say, from a conversation, or a note put through a friend's door. People see communication in a different light when they have to pay for it.

Other books can give you more factual detail than we are able to offer in the space available to us – but we think it is worth getting the main picture of what is going on.

Our media of mass communication are largely owned and run by corporations, a few of them state corporations, most business. Many of these corporations work on an international basis. All of them own pieces of a variety of media industries. The immediate result of this is that they often (but not always) think in terms of large audiences and large profits. And the result of this situation is that they will often produce material which, in order to have a mass appeal, works to a formula. In particular, there is a desire to appeal to the American market, for two reasons. One is that the USA spends more money on communication products (especially entertainment) than any other country in the world. The other is that the Americans have such a well-developed system for distributing and marketing communication (among other products) that it pays to keep in with them. Events such as the Cannes Film Festival or the London VideoCom Fair are used by corporations to sell communications products on an international basis.

For example, in the United Kingdom, Thorn Electrical Industries own EMI. EMI owns a percentage of local radio and half of Thames Television. It has interests in electrical and sports industries. It owns the world's largest record company, with, of course, an audio cassette tape division. It markets blank and recorded video cassettes. Some of these have films on them. These films are there because it runs a film distribution network at home and abroad. It also owns over a hundred cinemas in all major UK cities. It finances films.

And the ramifications do not stop there. EMI has a long-standing deal with Columbia Pictures to handle its films in Britain. And then again, Columbia is owned by the Coca Cola Company.

Clearly this network of alliances and of ownership not only typifies the source of communication in the mass media, but also says something about their power. It helps us interpret as well as describe. It helps explain why the media sell a lot of entertainment product – it is profitable. As we have said, it helps explain a certain lack of variety in the types of communication product. It helps explain the ability of these owners to market and promote their products as heavily as they do.

This leads naturally to considerations of finance. Who pays, and how?

One simple answer is that the audience always pays – at the box office, through the cover price, at the counter, through the licence fee, through the goods they buy.

That kind of financing represents no control, other than in the crudest terms, over what is bought. But the immediate financiers may have a powerful control over the communication that we buy. This is why, once more, it is worth describing the situation broadly, so that one can then interpret it in terms of consequences. There are two immediate sources of finance for most examples one can think of.

One is the direct finance that comes from the owning company or its backing bankers. And the cost of media operations is so huge that it is not surprising that the owners have to be what we would call 'big business'. In 1984 it cost an average of £200,000 to produce one hour of drama for television. Hardly surprising, then, that Granada obtained American co-production money to finance the twelve hours of a recent drama serial, *The Jewel in the Crown*. And the effect of this is to concentrate power further in the hands of those producers who do have money (and so reinforce their kind of material), and to lock out anyone with ideas about doing something different. Lest our picture looks too desperate, it should be pointed out that, for example, Channel Four in the United Kingdom has been set up in such a way as to allow smaller companies to get some of their productions onto the screen. Similarly, American public-service channels also serve minority audiences. They provide some sort of alternative to the mass commercial product.

But then there is the second main source of finance – advertising. Advertisers pay heavily for a special kind of communication, and expect to see results. They may themselves be large companies, with a good deal of financial muscle. And, for example, a magazine advertisement for lipstick sells not only because of the persuasive skill of the advertisement, but also as a result of the communication in the rest of the magazine. So one obvious effect of this source of finance is that the magazine producers tend to produce the kind of material that will please the advertisers – material which sells to the target audience that the advertisers are aiming at. No one needs to twist the arms of the magazine owners. If they don't sell copies then their marketing division cannot prove to the lipstick manufacturers that it is worth paying to advertise in their magazine. No income, no magazine.

So the matter of who pays for the communication does affect the content and treatment of the communication that we get. Our magazine example is bound to put in feature articles about make-up, which, like the advertisement, suggest that lipstick makes you more attractive.

This in itself reinforces a certain way of looking at things, a certain sense of what is 'normal'. And so it would seem that, in our example, the communication is about more than lipsticks and the idea of what is attractive.

2.5 Overt and covert values

In fact, the media often communicate messages about beliefs and opinions. These stand for values – notions to do with good and bad, for and against, proper and improper, and so on.

These values may be very obviously stated. The 'Vote Labour' headline on the front of the UK *Daily Mirror* a few elections ago let one know pretty clearly the opinions of that newspaper.

But some of these values are not obvious or overt. They may be hidden or covert. Just how hidden is a matter of opinion, depending on a particular piece of communication, and on how perceptive its receivers are. But still the idea of covert values is a useful one for interpreting the media. It should cause us to look more closely at what is really said, and how.

It should also be said that those producing the piece of communication may or may not have intended to conceal certain messages.

In the example of an advertisement, it is likely that there is an intention to conceal. Those who construct advertisements are skilled communicators. They are aware that a product can best be sold on the back of an idea, and that idea should fit in with the audience's existing beliefs and values. But the idea mustn't be too obvious. For instance, there are at the moment a number of advertisements selling food products in association with the idea of health. So far, this is fairly plain: the value of good health is expressed as an overt value, in the case of all those advertisements for items like butter, bread, orange juice and yoghurt. But you now may recollect that many of these advertisements also show the product being consumed by families and, even more specifically, being served by the wife or mother. The covert value and message is that families are OK, and a good family buys and consumes the product. Also, advertisements for food, like many others, trade in covert messages about guilt and pleasure. A contemporary UK advert for cream advertises the product as 'naughty but nice!'.

To take another example, crime thrillers are always popular on television and radio and in the cinema. In particular, there is an English series called *The Professionals*, which is about two agents of a special secret government branch, who, of course, catch criminals of a political flavour and bring them to a sticky end. And here is the first point – they are hardly ever seen to bring them to justice. Indeed, one of the points of the series is that the special service operates outside most legal restrictions. In some, though not all of the series, the covert message is that the law is a mere inconvenience, and sometimes a downright hindrance. Much the same message came across in a best-selling film called *Dirty Harry*. Here the law was shown to shield a psychotic killer from justice on a mere technicality. In either case, the point about legal safeguards and protection is brushed aside.

Both the film and *The Professionals* carry a message about violence. The covert message is that violence is fairly acceptable if the hero carries a badge of office, and the victim is 'obviously' a criminal/pervert/political trouble-maker anyway. (There is also the matter of how the criminals are 'set up' by the story telling.)

These remarks certainly need not be taken as a total condemnation of both examples. But they do provide good examples of covert messages, which this time may indeed be unintentional.

Equally, we are suggesting that such covert messages do need to be looked for, debated and condemned if they are presenting values which are unacceptable to ourselves and/or to our society.

And in this process of analysis and interpretation we may also come across interesting contradictions in the covert values – and in our society's values in general. For example, in the case just given, we might assume that everyone would say that they believe in the rule of law. This is meant to protect us from the behaviour of unsocial individuals – those we might call criminals. But at the same time, we also believe in the right of individuals to 'do their own thing', and to preserve their own sense of what is right and wrong – a sense of 'natural' justice, perhaps. The works we referred to present a contradiction between natural justice and legal justice, between an individual's needs and the needs of society.

So there are covert messages in most examples of media communication. These messages are dominantly about values. The values are to do with the meaning of the communication. These meanings have more or less significance according to obvious factors like what is said, who says it, who is receiving the message, and how many times it is repeated.

2.6 Stereotypes

A stereotype of a person is based on repeated description and ideas. A stereotype stands for a set of people, like women or businessmen, and is supposed to typify that set.

A stereotype is a simplification. It is not only about appearance, but also to do with relationships and beliefs connected with the type of person. In effect, it adds up to a snap description and an uncritical judgement of that person.

There are many well-known stereotypes of women, such as the so-called dumb blonde. But people are also typed in terms of things like race and religion. Some stereotypes are actually meant to be insulting – the image of the mean Scotsman or Jew. In fact, most stereotypes are insulting in some way, and all are a kind of evasion of the real complexity and interest of complete human beings.

The media use stereotypes of people as a kind of shorthand for getting their messages across. It is easier to represent a stereotype than to describe and build a full character. But while the media are guilty of reinforcing stereotypes, they have not invented them. They use them because it is known that they are used and understood by society in general. They offer an easy point of contact. The worrying thing is that stereotypes are also often a collection of prejudices. In this sense the power of the media becomes destructive because in repeating stereotypes they are therefore repeating prejudices on a grand scale.

For example, comedy is full of stereotypes. We are certainly not in the business of damning all comedy because of this. But we are, saying that much comedy communicates through stereotypes, and that this is not always a good thing. There are arguments about comedy releasing tensions and helping people come together. But some comedy around the stereotype of the mother-in-law is likely to create tension in those ladies, rather than release it. Similarly, if one belonged to the Chinese community then the exaggerated voices in some radio comedy could be rather irritating. And on television, if one was male and gay, then the exaggerated limp-wrist style of some comedy stereotypes would also be pretty infuriating.

Stereotypes predominate in fiction material. But they are by no means exclusive to comedy. Boys' comics represent stereotypes of square-jawed war heroes. Horror movies represent swooning female stereotypes in nighties. Romantic novels represent stereotyped heroes. One type, for example, is middle class, male and masterful. He has the power that comes from his work and social position, and can sweep the female off to exotic places. In short, he represents a fantasy, but a fantasy with a narrow range of ideas.

So, in one sense stereotypes are a device for sketching in a character quickly. In another sense they may be a device for appealing to the audience's existing attitudes and beliefs, and indeed, prejudices. They certainly do communicate values to the audience and appear to have the effect at least of reinforcing those attitudes and beliefs.

Because they are so easily recognizable, stereotypes are, to an extent, commercial. That is to say, if they are attractive or popular, and quickly recognized, then they will probably sell. The Benny Hill show may upset a number of people with its stereotyped treatment of female sexual features, but it scores good television ratings in England and in the United States. And, as we have said, people's awareness of these stereotypes is heightened and reinforced through media powers of repetition and penetration.

2.7 Genres

This same process of repetition also reinforces the popularity of identifiable forms of media product called genres.

The main idea of genre incorporates a story form in any one of the media, including repeated elements like stock characters and situations. Science fiction stories or cop thrillers are genres. But the idea of genre may also be extended to identify other repetitive types of media product.

For example, television quiz shows may be said to be a genre because they also work to a formula. They are always about competition, often for a prize. They always have the same hero figure – the ever-smiling compère. They often have young, glamorous women as stock characters, usually to give away prizes. The backgrounds are frequently the same – garish, theatrical sets. And they even have a kind of repeated story line which involves the compère as narrator raising the tension until the climax at the end, when a winner is announced and rewarded. At the time of writing, a UK quiz show, *The Price is Right*, hit peak viewing figures for one week: 16 million. Ask yourself why this happened. What is it about such shows that makes them so popular?

The word genre helps us to interpret the media because it helps identify a dominant type of media product. It leads us to the repeated elements and then to the messages that are within the stories of genre. For instance, the quiz show's message is something about the importance of competing to get what you want, and about wanting to have material possessions.

The media often communicate through the genre formula.

But it is no accident that genres develop. They are popular. And it is not surprising that they also use types and stereotypes in their characterization. Genres are a dominant type of media entertainment because they are popular, and therefore profitable. Stereotypes are part of that popularity.

In the case of either the genre or the stereotype, the point of contact through the communication is immediate and powerful. An extreme example of this can be summed up in three words – a poncho, a cheroot and a gun. Verbally or visually this adds up to the image of Clint Eastwood, a type of Western hero in a type of film, the spaghetti western. Any communication sign that can achieve this degree of recognition across such a wide area of the globe must have power. Such power suggests influence as well as popularity.

The significance of the influence of a piece of genre material depends on what one believes its messages to be, as well as on one's point of view. But in particular, genres often represent the main beliefs and values of the culture that makes them at a given time. And in turn the genres also confirm those values as they represent them. The problem is to be objective enough about the communication process to be able to stand back and see what is going on. For example, it is now fairly obvious that the number of spy, Western and science fiction films of the 1950s that were about invasions and threats to American society, were actually about the high degree of anxiety about communism and Russia at the time. Not so many people saw this then. But when we bring together terms like genre, repetition and covert values as tools for opening up the meaning of examples of media communication, then we have a better chance of working out what that meaning is.

The unwritten rules of what elements are expected to be in a given genre and of how they are expected to be used are called conventions. We have used the same word to describe the rules which bind the use of signs within codes of communication. So it is a word which is strongly applicable to genre, but not unique to it. What is useful about the term is that it promotes the idea that there are rules. This draws attention to the fact, once more, that we do not make and understand pieces of communication by chance. We can control our production of communication if we choose to. We can also be more precise about understanding the meaning of what is communicated, if we make the effort.

One example of a convention which works on genre material is that which says that the hero must appear within the first five minutes, if not sooner. It is a way of getting the audience to identify and possibly sympathize with the hero at an early stage of the story. But of course it is only a convention. It is not an absolute rule or law of nature. Conventions in genres change and adapt as the genres themselves are used again and again. Try watching a genre thriller serial with the sound down. You should still be able to identify the heroes and villains. Why and how?

Comment

At this point we would remind you of the theory of terms offered in chapter 1. These should also help you interpret the process through which the media communicate with us.

For example, you might notice the relative lack of feedback.

Reference was made to advertising and its intention of changing our behaviour.

See if you can identify some of the codes which television uses in its communication with us.

3 THE MEDIA: PARTICULAR EXAMPLES

No story!

But look carefully at the advertisement for Software Limited and decide what you would say about its source, its message and its audience before reading on.

About the advertisement: Software Limited

We want to analyse this advertisement mainly with reference to the picture. It is fairly typical of a full-page advertisement in that more than half the area is pictorial or graphic. You will find an account of image analysis in the section on images. This is how these ideas help bring out the meanings in this picture.

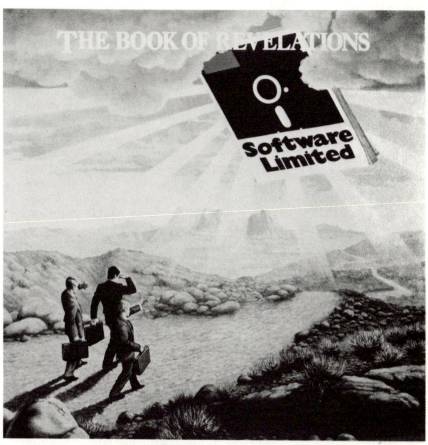

THE BOOK OF REVELATIONS

How do you see the role of the software you buy? Could your view be perhaps too narrow? If so, your business may not be benefitting fully from your hardware investment.

At Software Limited, we publish a catalogue that will shine a bright, broad light on the possibilities open to you.

We believe it's the most comprehensive and detailed catalogue available. In short, the state of the art today.

Armed with this information, and with the expert individual guidance Software personnel can offer, you've got a winning combination to set your business on the right road.

And that could be a revelation.

More to choose from
The only choice to make

Telephone 01 833 1173/6
01 833 2601/2   01 278 1371/2

No 2 Alice Owen Technology Centre
251 Goswell Road, London EC1N 7JQ

Operating Systems: CP/M 80, CP/M 86, MS DOS & PC DOS

Illustration G Advertisement – decoding signs and meanings

Camera position: places us as if on a hillside overlooking the scene. We are secret and spying on the moment of revelation through a 'magic window'. This is a view typical of fiction-film camerawork. Because it is typical, it is familiar and acceptable.

Image elements: the composition of the picture is dominated by two focal points, the men and the 'book' are both darker in tone than the rest of the picture. Attention is further drawn to the 'book' by the light rays. This is a realist drawing, with devices such as foregrounding and shading used to make the scene appear to have depth. Foregrounding also helps draw attention to the 'book'. The lighting helps emphasize the men (customers) and the 'book' (solution to the customers' problems). The men have dark shadows behind them, the dark book is set against a pale background. So there are many signs telling us what is important and what to pay attention to. The frame cuts off the scene as if there is a world continuing outside it: this is part of the camera view as well, a view that we have come to accept as natural.

Image content: we have referred to the fact that the audience for the product is identified and depicted in the image. Most obviously, the background and view of men walking along a road refers to the biblical story identified by the caption. This is a revelation like St Paul's on the road to Damascus. The countryside is that of the arid Middle East. The 'book' revealed in the sky echoes 2000 years of Christian stories and paintings showing, for example, the hand of God descending through clouds. In other words the content of this image is quite culture-specific in the way it produces meanings. The meaning is not so much in the individual items of content, as in the way that they are arranged to tell a story and to remind the western viewer of a particular kind of story.

This advertisement, like many others, uses stereotypes. The three figures are quickly identified as male business executives. What visual details point up this stereotype?

Anchorage: the metaphor or theme of the picture (Software equals a divine revelation) is anchored by the white caption. It supports the image. It ties it down. There is play on the literal and the biblical sense of the word revelation. But the real point and source of the advertisement is anchored by the company title and logo on the book in the sky.

Other: it is worth pointing out that however dominant the picture is, it is only part of the whole piece of communication. Notice for example the deliberate repetition of the company logo. Also notice how the copy plays on the theme – 'shine a bright, broad light'; 'set your business on the right road'.

There may well be other points that you could comment on. For example, do you see any significance in the typefaces used in the picture? Is the fact that there are *three* businessmen significant? Do you think the advertisement contains any elements of humour? Might some people dislike the religious comparison?

3.1 Advertising

Stereotypes

We have already explained the concept of stereotypes in the previous section.

Advertising tends to exploit the use of stereotypes because it has to communicate very quickly with its audience. As we have noted, stereotypes are immediately recognizable. If the advertisement has to sketch in a situation rapidly, then it helps to be able to slot characters into instantly recognizable roles. Stereotypes are all about instant roles.

Advertisers also like to identify their target audience as a group in the advertisement – 'busy housewives', 'Martini people'. So again, stereotypes help do this.

It is also arguable that advertising is especially responsible for maintaining and fixing stereotypes in the public consciousness. Very simply, advertising campaigns work across a range of media. Advertisements are repeated many times. Apart from genres they are the most repetitious use of communication in the media. So anything that they say, many times, is likely to get known. Even something as unglamorous as a National Savings Certificate scheme becomes indelibly printed on our consciousness as 'Grannybonds'.

And remember that the stereotyping is not just about role and appearance, but also about relationships and situations. There are no unmarried mothers in advertisements, no arguments between parents and children, and people are mostly at home or at play. There are a lot of large, well-appointed cars and large, well-appointed homes.

Covert messages

Indeed, these stereotypes of people and their situations also stand for messages about values, about a way of life and a set of beliefs that we in turn are invited to believe in. We have already given an advertising example for this concept. And we said then that the degree of covertness or overtness in these messages is a matter of observation and opinion.

But consider one more example. There is the value of 'newness'. Think of the number of advertisements which sell the product using the word new, or by emphasizing this is the 'latest model', or by emphasizing the glossy new appearance of the product, or by giving some space age context to the product. All this adds up to the covert message that newness is OK. If it is new, it must be good. This is, of course, convenient to manufacturers competing in markets that are already saturated with a given product and where there isn't much new to offer the public. But it does also mean that we may come to believe in newness for the sake of it. Something new is not necessarily a good thing. It is just – new.

Alternative realities

Apart from covert values, advertisements often communicate to us an idea of alternative realities. These are other situations and lifestyles. Some commentators have talked of an alternative world of the media. The idea of something manufactured is still there. But it is most accurate to recognize that what advertising communicates to us is a set of complementary fantasies.

These alternative realities are best recognized through the backgrounds in the advertisements. For instance, there is the 'beach in the sun' fantasy, including tropical islands, which has been used to give a context to the sale of products like holidays, crisps, drinks, sweets. Not all advertisements fit the patterns, but enough to make the patterns valid. Again, there is the alternative 'ideal home'. This home has its downmarket and upmarket versions, and is usually shown in separate, disconnected rooms. But it is there, behind cleaning products for kitchen and bathroom, or types of fire and drinks for the living room, or furnishings for the bedroom.

Look for these alternative realities yourself. Construct them for yourself from magazine pictures. You will find other versions such as 'action in foreign parts', the traditional English countryside, the high-tech office, and so on.

The point is that the advertisements promote the illusion that these alternative backgrounds and situations are real. They are not. They are mostly myths about different worlds that the advertisers (and perhaps ourselves) would like to exist. The communication is the result of a careful process of construction, to enhance the illusion. Once more, it carries messages about values which are artificially enhanced by advertising. For example, the English countryside world is also about nostalgia for another way of life (which in any case never existed as it's depicted). We buy the dream of a lost world when we buy the product.

Advertising as communication

This is to underline the fact that an advertisement is no more or less than another piece of communication. It has an opening tease like any story to gain attention. It develops its own ideas and message in its main part, like a story. And it concludes with a punch line or a twist, like a story – anything to make its message memorable. **Advertising is an example of communication that is very consciously planned.** It is presented with the intention of affecting the audience. Television advertising is an example of communication that is notable in terms of its costs.

On British television a twenty-five-second advertisement can cost £30,000 or more to make, and £60,000 or more to transmit on peak time slots over the whole TV network for a week. In terms of campaigns, covering a range of media for say, two months, it would cost at least £1 million to give a major new product in the domestic consumer market a proper launch.

But still, advertising is only communication. The process by which it communicates is susceptible to analysis, as with any other example.

When we examine the **source** of the message we notice the interesting fact that it is in three parts. The advertising agency, or creative consultancy, may create the message. But the client for whom the advertisement is made also pays for it, and has some say in what goes into the advert. And the media that present the advert are also a source, so far as the audience is concerned. Their time slot or page space has to be paid for. And indeed, local display advertisements (the boxed ones with pictures) in local newspapers are mostly produced by the paper's own team. Similarly, local television makes solely local advertisements for local businesses.

If we examine the idea of **audience**, then we notice that advertisers, while bearing in mind that they want to communicate with fairly large numbers of people, still try to specify a typical member of their target audience as tightly as possible. The agency will produce an imaginative description of such a person. This will include all the attributes that we perceive in others – age, occupation, status and so on, as well as ideas about their lifestyle. They are careful about who they think they are talking to, and adjust their communication style accordingly. Ineffective communication is expensive.

In the same way, the advertiser thinks about the characteristics of the **medium** that he is using, about its possibilities.

And he is well aware of the social **context** within which he is operating. Advertisements fall within the consensus of our beliefs and values. They exploit them. They would never oppose them. In addition, they are sensitive to cultural nuances within the social mix, especially as they apply to particular groups of consumers. Advertisements for clothes for young people, for example, are alert to changing habits and fashions out in the real world. They follow at a safe distance behind, but they are there. A current example of this is the way that New York street dancing, breakdancing, has firstly been taken up by popular cinema and is now being incorporated in advertisements for clothes and other products for the young market.

Categories of advertisements

Advertisements are usually divided into two broad categories: classified and display.

Classified advertisements are those lists of small ads in columns at the back of newspapers and magazines. They are used for recruiting staff as well as for selling and publicizing products and services.

Job advertisements usually include the job title, duties and responsibilities, expected qualifications and experience of the person wanted, some idea of salary, conditions including any fringe benefits.

Display advertisements include all press, radio, cinema, TV and outdoor advertising which seeks to display the product or service to potential buyers. In general, classified advertisements are more factual and brief. Display advertisements may contain facts about the goods but are intended to be more persuasive and attractive. It has been suggested that a display advertisement should achieve four purposes:

attract *attention*,
arouse *interest*,
create *desire*,
and lead to *action*.

Look at and listen to some ads, to see how far they seek to do all four things. In most modern advertisements the action part is left unstated.

Brochures are also an interesting example of advertising and publicity which are produced in a great variety of styles from almost all business organizations. We suggest you collect some and analyse them as pieces of communication.

3.2 Visual communication

Definitions

Many forms and media of communication are coded and decoded through the use of the eye, including writing.

But in practice, by visual communication we refer only to those means of communication which use clearly pictorial or graphic elements. However, it must be recognized that media can contain graphic elements even in their treatment of the printed words. For example, popular newspapers are certainly visual media, not only because of the high proportion of pictures in them, but also because of the intensely graphic treatment of print (banner headlines, varied typeface and type size and so on).

Having made these points, it is now possible **to divide visual communication broadly into representational and the schematic modes**. Representational visuals purport to look like the thing they represent. Most magazine and news photographs are of this mode.

But schematic visuals, while they communicate visually, don't pretend to be anything but symbolic. A lot of what we think of as graphics are of this mode – bar charts, pie charts and the like.

This is a useful division. It will not fit every single case. And some examples could seem to be a bit of both. You should look around you at the enormous variety of visual communication in our environment (street signs for example), and make your own mind up about particular instances.

We want to concentrate here on representational and photographic images. This is because such images dominate the range of mass media, with the obvious exception of radio. Visual communication is a dominant experience in our culture. And, because representational images do look like the thing they stand for, they are absorbed into our consciousness with a kind of immediacy and force that the written or spoken word lacks.

This is not to claim that one form of communication is better than the other – merely different.

Image reading

Images are composed of signs as much as any other form or medium. We learn to decode these signs when we learn to decode those other sound signs made by adults, called speech. Visual communication does not possess the precise sense of grammar and syntax that verbal communication does. But it does have conventions that for example predict the order of shots in a piece of film. We want to concentrate on the single image.

The signs through which we read images fall into three areas. First, there are the **position signs**.

These are signs given by the placing of the camera (or artist's point of view). How close the camera is to what it depicts (proximity), and the angle that it takes, defines how we understand the image. This is about the meaning of the signs. The position of the camera defines our position as spectator. It becomes our position. For example, you will find that in many advertisements the camera actually directs attention to the product, though this may be a small part of the whole image. Or, if a woman is being used to sell the product, the camera directs attention to her sexuality. There is a pretty well-known advertisement for a bath product in which we are positioned in a room behind a half-naked woman in the foreground. The camera sign means, pay attention to this.

Next there are the **image structure signs**. These are elements from which the image is put together:

Composition is about where items are placed in the frame.

Framing is about the border, what it encloses, what it excludes.

Colour is about overall hues, or the selective placing of colour within the frame.

Foregrounding is about placing objects in the front of the frame, and so making them larger (this is also a sign of the supposed three dimensionality of an image – a visual 'trick').

Middleground and *background* is about placing objects in relation to foreground, and also saying something about their importance.

Lighting is about things like picking out or diminishing objects according to how well lit they are. It is also about ideas of style.

Focus is about what is made clear or unclear through choice and use of camera lens. This also may sign to us to direct our attention towards a certain object. Or it could sign something like, this is a dream or fantasy picture.

Perspective devices (relative size of objects – lines of ceiling or floor) are about the illusion of depth in an image. We learn to read such signs as 'depth'. An image, of course, has no depth.

Next, there are **image content signs**.

These are simply the objects within the frame. In fact we have learnt to believe they are there because of various other signs that are part of the process of visual perception – shape, outline, hue, tone. But if we accept that they are so identified, then the objects themselves may sign to us, especially in combination. One visual cliché is the young girl and the apple, meant to sign health. This example is useful because it also reminds us that objects can become symbols in an image. In this case, there is an additional tinge of tease and sexuality because the two objects stand for more than just what they are. They also stand for the story of temptation in the Garden of Eden and all the associations that this has.

You may be able to add to these signs, and certainly to the examples. But the point about the three areas remains, as does the basic point that the meaning of the image is not natural, but is constructed by the image makers through the use of these signs. We understand the code. If we didn't we couldn't make sense of what we were looking at.

The overall meaning of the image is confirmed by our reference to all the signs. Two or three on their own may not be enough. In any case the meaning of most images is actually quite complex. It can take many words to explain a picture.

And the point of image reading is to get to the total possible meanings of the image. Often we are very careless about decoding images, either in not getting the full meaning or in not realizing that we are getting covert messages. It is commonly thought that pictures are 'easy to read'. This is questionable. But in any case, this doesn't mean to say that they are simple.

A visual medium like television can offer us multiple codes of communication – visual, non-verbal, written captions, the spoken word and so on. So there is a complex variety of signs giving us the message.

Socialization and beliefs

Images are especially powerful in offering messages about beliefs because they are a dominant channel of communication in the media.

You should also refer back to what we said about the power of the mass media in general. For the same reasons they are also a powerful agent of socialization. Socialization describes the ways in which we are taught or learn to fit into society. This includes society in general, as well as particular parts of society. Obviously, for example, one's family is also an agent of socialization – we learn from our growing experience in the family. We learn ways of behaving, a way of looking at the world, sets of beliefs and values.

Images on television or in magazines, for instance, are influential because they offer direct models. That is, we can see what we could look like, how we could behave, how we could relate to others – everything is illustrated for us. It is all there in the pictures. For example, there are certain pictures that say a lot to us about the importance of security. Insurance company advertisements are inclined to promote this value because their business is based on it. But one would also be able to find a wide variety of other media material which represented the security of the home, the security of having savings, the security of having long-term relationships.

The idea of socialization relates to the notion of security as follows. One sees images of social behaviour and social relationships, in which security figures. The insurance company advertisement may suggest that one is a good husband and a proper husband if one insures one's life, and the loving wife and family are there as a reward. DIY magazines present images of homes made more physically secure. Newspapers often represent disapprovingly those who appear to threaten security in the family or the work place or in society as a whole – strikers would be the obvious example here.

Denotation, connotation, anchorage

You may come across these three terms which are also used to help explain how images communicate and how we may analyse them. **Denotation** is about image content – see our image reading section above (p. 180). The idea is that one should look very carefully at everything that is in the image, and describe what it is and how it is treated. The idea is to stop one taking the quick and casual glance that we give to so many images around us – posters, for example.

Connotation is about image meaning. The idea is that one can then take the content carefully described, and work out the meaning of the parts and the whole. The meaning will result from personal and cultural associations and experiences which we more or less share. Once more, the intention is to get the whole meaning, not just a partial one: to get the covert messages as well as the overt ones.

Anchorage is about particular aspects of an image which help pin down (or anchor) its meaning. Newspaper photographs are anchored by their captions – these help pin down, for example, who a person is and what they are doing. Advertisements may be anchored by a logo, a slogan, or the presence of the product somewhere in the image. Try cutting out newspaper photographs without their captions. How do the meanings change? Then add your own captions. Now what are the connotations of the image as anchored by your words?

A comment on storyboards

Storyboards, which are used for initial planning of slide-tape sequences and films, are worth noting at this point. To create an audio-visual production it is useful to visualize the picture sequence before filming or photographing takes place. A storyboard is a numbered series of simple sketches which show the producer and/or the person who commissioned the production how the sequence of film shots or slides will look. The drawings can simply be matchstick figures or line backgrounds sufficient to indicate the type of visual image.

Having created this basic storyboard it is necessary to relate sound to these pictures (even a 'silent film' normally includes music). Usually a separate script is written with details of visuals and sound. It is, however, possible to create a storyboard which includes some of the sound script (words/music) alongside the appropriate picture.

In the final production script there would be four components: first, the number of each different shot or frame (which corresponds to the numbers of the storyboard pictures); second, picture instructions to fulfil the storyboard idea (e.g. close-up on face, long shot of ear); third, sound details (music, effects, dialogue or narrative); fourth, the running time for each shot to plan the total length of the production.

Production notes may also accompany such a script. These could include points about location of filming, instructions for camera shots, editing, props required, mix of music and dialogue.

Storyboards, scripts and production notes are all documents for planning and organizing the team of people who will create the finished product. Such preparations are required whether the product is a training film, a slide sequence for publicity or, indeed, an art film.

Figure 27 provides an example of a storyboard.

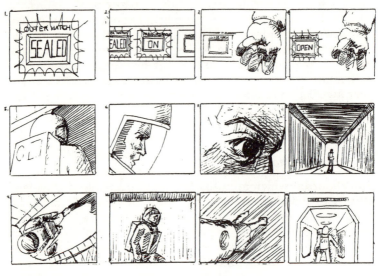

Script to accompany storyboard

Shot	Picture	Sound	Time
1	INTERIOR: SPACESHIP AIRLOCK ECU on flashing indicator. Then	General atmosphere. Click of lock and rush of air.	
2	TRACK &		12 secs
3	PULL BACK to show clenched hand foreground.		
4	ANGLE on same. Shows Inner Hatch Open sign.	Hatch signal bleeps.	2 secs
5	MCU. Low angle behind suited astronaut as hatch rises.	Humming of motor. Astronaut breathing.	2 secs
6	CU Astronaut's helmeted face in profile.	Humming stops. Breathing continues.	2 secs
7	ECU Astronaut's eye from side.	Atmosphere only.	2 secs
8	INT.: SPACESHIP CORRIDOR. MLS along corridor to show astronaut backlit. Low POV emphasizes perspective.	Atmosphere ASTRONAUT: 'It's empty. I'm going inside.'	3 secs
9	MS from above astronaut entering corridor.	Muffled footsteps. ASTRONAUT: 'No one.'	2 secs
10	MS from side. Astronaut walks down corridor.	FX as before. ASTRONAUT: 'I can't see a thing in here. Wait a minute!'	3 secs

Figure 27   Storyboard – pre-title sequence for a sci-fi film

3.3 News

Construction of reality

News and current affairs material is crucial in constructing our view of the world. This view is mainly a combination of information and beliefs. That is, what we think are the facts about the world we live in, and what beliefs and values we have which organize those facts. So we are talking about what we believe the world to be like. But our country, other countries, other ways of life, all look different depending on what point of view one starts from. The media help shape that point of view.

The news is especially influential, not only because it comes through powerful media, but also because it is believed. And we believe television and radio news in particular because much of what is said is factually true, and because the news organizations have spent many years promoting their reputation for truthfulness and impartiality. However, given the necessary process of selection and construction which is part of news making, it is impossible for the news makers to provide the whole truth or a complete view of the world. They will interpret wars, disasters and affairs of state in the way that seems most truthful to them. This will be their view of the world. It is in effect offered to us and becomes part of our reality.

For example, members of some factions fighting in the Middle East have been referred to as 'terrorists' and the disapproving comments of politicians have been widely reported. But the news makers of some Middle Eastern countries have called those same people 'freedom fighters' and have quoted favourable comment. Neither view may be entirely right or wrong. But in both cases we are seeing views promoted, as much as facts reported. In each case, the view of the world believed by the news makers becomes part of the communication to the audience. And in each case, they are contributing a little more to each audience's sense of reality.

They are helping construct a reality which is made up of beliefs as well as facts.

Agenda setting

This phrase means that **the news makers in various media promote a list of the most important news topics** (in the same way that an agenda of topics is set for a meeting). This list can be argued over in detail, but it certainly includes stories about political events, about disasters, about war, about the royal family and about popular public figures. You should also refer here to the next section on news values.

This list is of general topic headings. But the agenda is actually about particular events of the moment that will probably come under these headings. As we write this, stories on the agenda include a long-running miners' strike and an explosion on an oil tanker. With a little thought, you can provide your own agenda as you read this.

If you can do this – identify those stories which are dominating the news media in a given week, then you are also identifying what the news makers consider to be important. In effect, they are telling you what is important. They may or may not be right. We don't know or don't notice those items which are dropped or given little space or time. Indeed, in this way they are 'said' to be less important. But still, the fact is that, positively or negatively, we are 'told' what is on the news agenda for the week. The idea that newspapers and news programmes simply communicate what is happening does not hold up. Messages, even news messages, are shaped in particular ways for particular reasons.

So the idea of an agenda is useful because it helps us interpret news as communication. If we notice the pattern that is the agenda, then we may ask who sets the agenda and what effect this might have. These are questions about source and audience. In the first case, we notice that it is an editorial team, influenced by their ideas of news value. In the second case, we notice that the audience is affected once more in the sense that their view of the world is being defined by communication that they receive from others. None of this is to suggest that news makers conspire to set the agenda. The fact that there is an agenda of broadly similar items most weeks is a result of their own similar backgrounds and views of what is 'real' and 'important'. Also, news reporters and editors use the same news agency sources and continually look at what each other is presenting. For instance, radio and television editors always look at the newspapers first thing in the morning.

So, if the news does help construct our reality, we are finding out more about how and why this is done.

News values

These values are accepted by the people who make the news. They are **beliefs about what topics make good news** and **beliefs about how those topics should be handled.**

The topics are those which we have already seen on the news agenda. The same sort of topics tend to appear every week in most media because people in news organizations believe that they are the right sort of topics to attract the audience into reading or watching. To a fair extent it seems that they are right. But we should also remember the point that, without trying alternatives, no one really knows what the audience might be interested in. Also, although there might be a kind of agreement about types of news story it is most important to present, this still doesn't prove that a particular story has to be chosen, or that it has to be treated in the way that news stories often are.

In fact, beliefs about the handling of topics are rather more important than beliefs about what is handled, we would suggest. 'It's not what you say, but the way that you say it.'

Dominantly, news stories are handled in terms of drama, conflict and visual qualities.

Dramatization means that the creators of the story prefer something exciting, with a main character around whom the action revolves. So, in a disaster story in a popular newspaper, for example, one might get not only the drama of action as a fire is fought and people rescued, but also one might get a photograph and special story angle on the fireman hero who carried three children to safety. (Perhaps he was a hero, but then it is likely that so were some of his workmates who performed deeds with less emotional 'pull' than rescuing children.)

Conflict is introduced into stories by having two opposing sides, preferably villains to oppose the heroes.

So, for example, many political stories on television are handled in terms of opposing views (as if there could not be more than two views on some event or issue). If the leader of one political party can be set up against the leader of another, so much the better. And labels are used to make it all simpler. At the time of writing we have had a number of stories in the United Kingdom about internal Tory party conflict between 'wets' and Thatcherites. It is as if there are only two kinds of Tory Member of Parliament. This is illogical.

This tendency to handle news in this way – a belief that it is right to handle it in this way – excludes shades of opinion. Its misleading effect needs to be seen in the light of the fact that relatively few people watch the current affairs programmes which might fill in the shades of opinion. If you look at news stories around you now, you will find various examples of this treatment – perhaps the police in conflict with some social group, for example. In this instance, it might well be demonstrators of some kind. Indeed, developing the old cliché that only bad news is good news, it could be said that peaceful demonstrations are bad news for the news people – there is neither drama nor conflict.

However, the third value of news handling might make a demonstration into a good story. It could provide lots of pictures. Television and popular newspapers have been made visual media, in a sense, because there is a preference for using picture material.

Television must have images of some sort, of course. But still, news makers will exploit this aspect of the medium by preferring stories with pictures and by sending out cameras to obtain picture material. Newspapers do a similar thing. As we have said, the story is put together, it doesn't just happen. Choices are made about how to handle it. And the use of a large picture of, for example, a personality arriving at an airport, with but a few words to say who and why, is definitely a choice. This choice represents a belief about what makes good news handling. This is the news value.

Gatekeeping

Among the team making the news, it is the sub-editor who has most responsibility for upholding news values, whether of content or of treatment. This person has the job of taking the general run of news stories, deciding whether they are news-worthy or not and then cutting or rewriting them as necessary to suit the newspaper and its page or the broadcast and its time slot.

People who handle information coming into an organiz-ation are called gatekeepers. The term also assumes that they have some power to decide who gets what information and sometimes to change some of it. People like receptionists and secretaries can be gatekeepers.

In this case of the news, the point that is being made is that indeed newsworthy material can be and is filtered and changed to suit the policies of the paper or broadcasting organization – to suit their values.

Clearly many other people can have an effect on the final content and treatment of the news. The editor, or section editors like the features editor, can also be influential and do some gate-keeping. But still the point is to draw attention to the fact that there is one group of people who are very influential in the process of message selection and message treatment – of the messages that we receive from the news programme or newspaper.

Editorializing

This term describes **the ways in which the broad opinions or points of view of the news making organization are expressed through the newspaper or programme**. Newspapers literally have an editorial – an article in which the editor expresses opinions on a number of news stories or issues raised by such stories. There is no question that newspapers do have a point of view. They have points of view defined in terms of their support for a political position or a political party. They may also have a position or attitudes towards matters that are not overtly political. For example, they may have particular attitudes towards conservation of the environment, or the outcome of a major legal case. So, newspapers cannot pretend to be unbiased. The kinds of bias or opinion that they have can be explored through investigation of covert messages revealed in patterns of content or treatment. For instance, it is generally acknowledged that the *Daily Mail* in the United Kingdom is angled towards an audience including a high proportion of females, and towards a position on the right of the political spectrum.

In the United Kingdom the case of broadcasting is rather different. News broadcasting does not editorialize in the way that a newspaper does. There are no editorials. Presentation of news items pays attention to the ideals of balance and impartiality.

Points of view should not be expressed on things that have happened, or on issues raised, especially political issues. The Acts of Parliament that brought into being the BBC and the Independent Broadcasting systems actually require this neutrality. ITN news is paid for by the commercial contracting companies, but none of them actually owns it. It is not a commercial organization itself. Many countries also follow this line of 'telling the news like it is' in news broadcasting. However, perfect balance and impartiality is impossible to achieve. Someone has to make choices about what will be presented as news. There are reasons behind the choices that are made. These reasons are based on values and opinions.

So, we would argue that news broadcasting, not surprisingly, can editorialize covertly. The very notion of balance itself is a matter of opinion. It suggests the image of a weighing device called a balance. This has two sides. But we have already pointed out that many issues and arguments have more than two sides.

And certain news items, for example those to do with sensitive political or military matters, are likely not to be handled in a balanced way. One of the most obvious examples here in Britain relates to the situation in Northern Ireland, where British troops are fighting the Irish Republican Army. There is a long list of news items and current affairs programmes which have been censored by the government or by the executives in the news organizations because they would have represented a Republican point of view. Indeed there has been a ban on any members of that organization appearing on television. (Other books on news making provide fuller evidence of this case.) The point is that one cannot talk about balance if the views of one side are privileged and the other side suppressed. It may well be that many people would agree with this handling of the news in this case. But we should not pretend that it is balanced news. In an indirect and covert way the news broadcasters are actually editorializing. By leaving things out or by weighting picture time and interviews in such a news item, they can present a point of view or a way of looking at that situation.

3.4 New technology

Definitions

This section is concerned with **micro-electronics and its effect on means of communication and systems of communication**. Sometimes old systems and means have been changed. Sometimes a new form or medium has been created.

The camera has been transformed as an object used to create visual communication: now it can set focus and exposure automatically. The telephone system is being transformed as new equipment controls the routing of electronic signals, passing via cables and satellites to most countries in the world, available from your home.

New communication devices like the video recorder have appeared. They are also changing our lifestyles, our culture and our ability to send and receive communication.

We want to draw attention to some of these devices and systems because they are having a considerable effect on our patterns of work and leisure and because, in many instances, these effects are taken for granted.

For example, a watch is a device for measuring time. For hundreds of years it has communicated that measurement through the symbols of two hands circling a dial marked with numbers. Suddenly there is a new generation which no longer has to learn these symbols. The digital watch communicates through number alone.

More to the point, new technology has made a watch so cheap that it is a throwaway object. Every child can have one.

A pocket calculator is a little more expensive. Yet its size and computing power would have made it a miracle even ten years ago.

And we are talking about a time scan that starts about ten years ago, but which extends into the foreseeable future. New technology has only just begun transforming our lives and our ability to communicate. Fresh surprises are round the corner, as scientists have begun creating objects such as the biochip that combines living tissue and electronics, and a computer that works with light rays instead of pulses of electricity. You can buy a 'solar-powered' pocket calculator in any shopping centre.

Effects on mass communication

New technology has extended the range of many means of mass communication.

It is now possible to talk to others around the world, from one's home. The development of the telephone system already referred to, together with link-ups with satellites and new cable systems has made all this possible.

And the most important development which has made it possible to connect these systems with each other and with computers has been the creation of technology that makes them all speak in the language of number – digital information.

For example, another extension is that of the electronic mail service, which connects computer users across continents, exchanging electronic letters instantly and at any time.

New technology has changed the production methods of many of the mass media in various ways. In general, it has made production quicker and cheaper and has improved the quality of what is produced.

For example, newspapers can now be put together by a few people using a sophisticated kind of word processor instead of a number of people putting together pieces of metal. Colour pictures in magazines and books can now be prepared by an electronic device that allows the printer to play around with the colours before deciding on the best version, instead of involving complicated efforts with photography and chemicals. Or a newspaper like the *Financial Times* (Europe) can be put together in Paris and the results sent along a wire to Frankfurt for printing.

New technology has brought new methods of distribution of material to the audience. In producers' terms, this means they can often get to a bigger market faster. For example, movies can now be distributed through cable systems such as Ten in England or Home Box Office in the United States, or through new devices like the video cassette.

New technology has widened the mass media access to their audience. For example, Sky Channel is broadcasting a new service to Europe via satellite and cable links.

New technology has created new products that are mass-produced for large audiences. For example, video games are now being marketed on a huge scale. The technology for the present games and their computers did not exist even five years ago.

Information

New technology has meant that systems of mass communication can handle more information faster than ever before.

Business organizations and governments have made the most use of this expensive information technology because it helps them save money or find new ways of making money. But still, all this affects us, even indirectly. It certainly affects most people in their work – for example, shop checkout tills that can also keep track of what stock is being sold.

In the United States, communication corporations offer nationwide services to business users, allowing them to pass written and graphic information from one business centre to another, via satellites. There is less and less paper moving around.

British banking is becoming computerized. Not only does this mean that customers can do things like take out money and check their accounts without going into a bank, but also it will soon mean that banks can stop moving paper cheques around altogether.

Data processing is now a commonly used phrase describing the ability of computer-based technology to store vast quantities of information about things like customers, stock and financial arrangements. This information can also be recovered quickly and moved around easily.

But here one should make at least some comment on the fact that such great changes in the communication of information have many effects, not all of them good. We are not going to make a lengthy analysis of social and economic effects, but two examples should indicate the scope of problems arising.

One point is that many people are losing jobs because of new technology. Apart from general production examples, like computerized lathes that can be 'taught' to operate without human hand, there is the loss of clerical jobs as files turn from the time-consuming paper systems to electronic stores. (Of course, new communications industries and jobs compensate for this situation to some extent.)

Another point could be the dangers of the computerized credit control agencies. These store information about many citizens, some of it personal and all related to their 'credit-worthiness'. At the moment it is impossible to control what is put on file and virtually impossible to see it and correct it. The power taken by those who operate new information systems is great, and the lack of checks on this power is worrying.

The issue of who gets to use and control new communication and information systems is a major one.

Entertainment

New technology has extended the range of mass-produced or mass-distributed entertainment.

A number of examples already given help prove this point. Entertainment is a big communications business. We pay for a lot of entertainment products. And as we have suggested already, this has other consequences when one considers the covert messages about values, or the reinforcement of culture and attitudes, that comes with this entertainment. For instance, video games are often designed around notions of competition, violence, war and the like: they are orientated towards young males and the values conventionally offered to this group through other media such as comics. In another example we can see how new developments tend to extend the scope and the tendencies of existing technology.

Portable personal tape recorders do for the audio tape medium what portable radio did for that medium a generation ago.

And all these extensions of entertainment are also an extension and diversification of the operation of existing media systems or media owners.

The home TV screen is now at the centre of a network of information and entertainment systems using a range of communication technologies. Figure 21 on page 131 originally appeared in the French magazine *L'Express* in August 1980 as part of an article entitled '*Notre télé, demain . . .*' (Our telly, tomorrow . . .).

How far do you consider this diagram of prediction has come into existence? Does your TV at home have any of these link-ups yet?

The mini screen within the main screen enables the viewer to monitor what's on other channels or other sources, such as the home surveillance camera.

Two issues

This brings us to the first of two issues with which new technology confronts us. **Are we going to get more of the same, or will we be offered something different?**

The immediate and regrettable answer is that, on the whole, new technology hasn't done much to change patterns of ownership, means of finance or the marketing of entertainment. In this sense, new developments tend to be absorbed by the existing systems and used in the way that they always have been. For instance the creation of video discs read by laser has enormous potential for creating a new kind of information store. In effect, these could be electronic books with moving pictures. Slow efforts are now being made in this direction. But what has actually happened with this technology in the first place is an attempt to see these discs mainly as pop records with pictures. Not surprisingly, given a successful video cassette market, this attempt has been a failure.

One other issue worth picking out is **the question of how much new technology will give us access to its new systems, or how much control we will have over what is offered to us.** Up to now we have been in a situation where mass communications systems and products have been effectively directed or controlled by commercial organizations, with some intervention by government. In other words, the messages are framed and sent to us without our having that much say about who does this and how. Given the large, complex and expensive operation of systems like a national telephone or television service, this is not to suggest that everyone can have a direct part in running them or producing material. At the same time it is also worth pointing out that, for example, the city of Hull runs a good, independent telephone service. Dutch broadcasting manages a system that gives minority groups some right to air time. It can be done. The fact that there are some pressures for alternative approaches to mass communication may be seen through examples in Britain. There are alternative local papers such as the *Hackney Gazette*. And it is admitted officially that there are some fifty illegal radio stations operating and serving particular areas or particular minority interests. Cheap technology makes it possible to run these operations on a shoestring.

So there are signs that rather more access and control for the audience or user is possible with new technology.

It is in the new cable systems and the applications of computers that one can see the best signs of this happening. Cables are being used to carry messages from the consumer as well as to them. For instance, in some areas of the United States and Britain it is possible to shop by cable, using a keyboard and display screen. Interactive video systems are now coming on the market (a video linked with a computer), which allow a student to learn at his or her own pace. Information relevant to professions such as the law is now being put on computer file to be retrieved by the professionals at work. It is now supposed that it will only be a matter of time before the whole of society is wired up and the population as a whole has the ability to get to more information more easily than ever.

But at this point of informed guesswork we must stop. It hasn't happened yet. And in the meantime, as we have suggested, there is still something to be desired in respect of our access to and use of mass communication, whatever the technological marvels that are now happening.

REVIEW

This is to help you check on the main points of this chapter, 'Mass communication'.

First, we have said that mass communication is about communication on a large scale, in terms of distance, people and product involved. Much of it is to do with the mass media. This is an important topic to study because of the potential influence that these media of communication have upon us.

1 A mass communication society.
1.1   The word 'mass' refers to the volume, scale or speed of the system, product or audience.

1.2 The significance of mass production of communication is that it also means the mass repetition of messages. The messages are sometimes about ideas and beliefs. These may influence us because they are so often repeated.

1.3 The systems or organizations of mass communication are not directly within our control as individuals, unlike face-to-face communication.

1.4 Mass communication has enabled more sending and exchange of information. But we are not necessarily able to control who sends what to us or what they do with information.

1.5 Mass communication has increased the range of entertainment available to us. But the choice of types of entertainment is not as great as it might appear. And we don't have much say in what we get.

1.6 The various means of mass communication can be seen as extensions of ourselves and of our abilities to do things like speaking, listening, writing, reading.

1.7 The media are part of our society in general. They help build up a picture of that society.

1.8 The media have power and influence within society because of their ability to duplicate and repeat messages and because of their ability to get to us, even into our homes.

2 Interpreting the media.

2.1 The idea of mediation refers to the way that material is changed by the workings of the media organizations. This is particularly relevant to media material that is about matters of fact.

2.2 Selection and construction refers to the way that any example of the media is the result of a process where items are picked, left out and put together in a certain way. One should then look at who does this, and why.

2.3 The idea of product refers to the fact that much media material is mass-produced like cars, and packaged and sold like breakfast cereal.

2.4 Ownership and finance refers to the source of media messages and to where they get the money from to pay for the operation. Ownership of the media tends to be dominated by relatively few organizations, mainly commercial interests. They are concerned with profitability above all and with increasing their dominant market position. In terms of finance, advertisers are especially dominant in influencing the kind of material we get, because they pay directly for a large proportion of media operations, even though the audience always pays in the end.

2.5 The idea of overt and covert values refers to the fact that intentionally or unintentionally not all messages in media material are obvious at first. They may be hidden. And the important messages are about values – beliefs and opinions.

2.6 The idea of stereotypes is that people, their behaviour and their beliefs are often represented in a simplified and misleading way in popular media material. They are easy to understand, but encourage prejudice and misunderstanding. Stereotypes are created through repetition of representation.

2.7 The idea of genres is that there are certain types of media material, often story types, which are also recognizable through repeated elements which go to make them up. Genres are popular. So one should look critically at covert messages that they may contain because they are also likely to be influential.

3 The media: particular examples.

3.1 Advertising: uses and perpetuates stereotypes; contains covert messages and values; creates alternative realities for its products and services; is a use of communication and may be analysed through communication terms.

3.2 Visual communication is a dominant means of communication in the mass media. In this sense it is mainly defined in terms of representational images, often the photograph. Images give meanings through signs which can be defined in terms of camera/viewer position, structure and content. Images socialize us into the system of beliefs and values that dominates our society by presenting that society to itself. Images can also be understood through terms like denotation, connotation and anchorage.

3.3 News is important, among other media material, because it brings us information about the world, which we use to construct our view of reality and truth. News makers set an agenda of topics which become the key issues and topics for us, the audience, at a given time. News makers have news values about what are important news topics and the 'right' ways to treat these topics. We tend to accept these values uncritically. The news machine illustrates the idea of gatekeeping in action, mainly through the selection and construction work done by sub-editors. News machines editorialize, overtly in newspapers, sometimes covertly in broadcasting: that is, they take positions on certain topics and issues. These points of view can represent kinds of political bias.

3.4 New technology, as defined through applications of micro-electronics, is changing mass communications systems, including the media and their products.

It has affected mass communication by extending its range, changing its production methods, bringing new distribution methods, extending access to the audience and creating new products. New technology has greatly increased our ability to exchange and store quantities of information. This has benefited government and commerce more than the general public. It has also raised issues such as the question of data control.

New technology has extended the range of mass entertainment. It has also raised many issues relating to media product, ownership and control. One crucial question is whether it can help bring us something different, or whether we will get more of the same. Another major question is whether or not we will have more access to use of communication systems as well as control of the material we get through them.

ACTIVITIES

1　For groups.
To find out how the mass media represent society to itself.
To investigate the notion of the alternative reality created by the media.
To illustrate the creation of 'types' in media images.

Use magazines as sources from which to cut out and mount images of people for display. Take one or both of two themes through which to make choices: one is the family; the other is the community. In each case you will find images that allow you to build up either a family tree or a community portrait gallery.

It is possible to take the exercise further by writing profiles for each of the 'characters' chosen. These profiles can include details of personality, background, attributes and lifestyle.

The fact that you will be able to do this fairly easily satisfies the three aims. But you might like to discuss these anyway and relate them to your picture displays.

2   For individuals or pairs.

To find out through practice how news material may be selected and reconstructed.

To understand the influence that news values may have on this process.

Read the following copy that might have come from a news agency such as Associated Press.

Coach Disaster – 14 killed   *(10.30 am, 27.8.84)*
A holiday coach returning to Britain from the French Riviera crashed near Ampiegne in northern France in the early hours of this morning.

The coach skidded off the main highway, N21, and plunged down an embankment before overturning. 11 of the 53 passengers were killed outright as the upper half of the coach was crushed. A further 3 passengers died on the way to hospital. Another 27 are being detained in the main hospital near Ampiegne. The extent of their injuries is not known as yet, though it is reported that at least 6 are on the critical list. The coach driver was among those killed.

The cause of the accident has not been established. A lorry driver who was at the scene of the accident said that roads were slippery with rain after a hot dry spell. The driver, M. Louis Gaspard, alerted French rescue and medical services through a CB radio that he carried in his cab. But for his prompt action in calling ambulances to the scene, the death toll might have been higher.

Mr Brian Ackroyd, a member of the British embassy staff in Paris, is now at Ampiegne, and providing assistance. The French Minister of Transport, M. Patrick Furneaux, has promised that there will be a full investigation into the causes of the crash. There have been other accidents on this stretch of road in the last year.

One of the few people to survive with only slight injuries was Mrs Amy Chalker. Her 3-year-old daughter, Mandy, also survived, after being flung through a skylight ripped from the roof of the coach. Mandy landed in a bush, only slightly bruised.

In view of a previous holiday coach crash last month, also in France, questions are likely to be raised about the speed at which the coach was travelling, and about the rules concerning drivers' working conditions.

You may assume that this copy could be accompanied by a wire picture showing the crashed coach. For television, there is also

Visnews coverage of the scene, plus an interview with the French lorry driver, whose English is reasonably good. You may not change the facts as outlined. You may elaborate plausibly, edit and impose style and angle on the material.

Your task is to do two things. One is to produce an article as for page 2 of a popular tabloid newspaper. The other is to script an item for a main television news programme, running for 1 minute 20 seconds. Remember to consider graphics and news film in this case.

You may also consider what this exercise tells you about the difference between the two media.

3   For individuals or groups.

To illustrate dominant patterns of ownership and finance in the media.

To illustrate the incorporation of new technology within these patterns.

(This exercise will either draw on your existing knowledge or it will require you to go to sources of information about your broadcasting system.)

Consider the following:

'A leading Japanese company is going to market a three-dimensional image video system. This produces apparently "real" images in the space of a 30 inch cube. The system is based on twin hologram discs and a laser player. The company intends to sell one system as it would video discs/players, with a library of material available to the purchaser.

'It is not possible to record on this system. The company is also negotiating with the main broadcasting organizations to allow the system to be used for broadcasting, at least on an experimental basis at first. So there are two possible applications for this new technology, one like video disc replay, the other like normal broadcasting.'

In each case, answer the following questions and reflect upon what your answers tell you about the way things are at the moment:

Who is likely to own the product in each case?

Who is likely to control the system?

How will each system be paid for?

Who is going to make money out of each system?

How might the player system be marketed?

(You can usefully go on to ask questions about what material is likely to be available or how the product might be censored.)

4 For pairs or groups.

To illustrate the existence of genre and the repetition of common elements.

To show the importance of conventions, and our hidden knowledge of these.

Simply, design a new television quiz show. The only condition is that there must be prizes. The details should include information about how it is run and presented, as much as facts about the quiz itself.

Compare your production with that of other people. You will probably find that they have a great deal in common. So then ask yourself why this is so and why it may be significant.

SUGGESTED READING

Morley, David, and Whitaker, Brian (eds), *The Press, Radio and TV: an introduction to the media.*
Hood, Stuart, *On Television.*
Tunstall, Jeremy, *The Media in Britain.*
See also the resources list at the end of the book.

GLOSSARY OF COMMUNICATION TERMS

This list provides a brief definition of how some important terms are used in communication studies. We also suggest you consult the Index of this book.

For further references and information see *Key Concepts in Communication*, by T. O'Sullivan, J. Hartley, D. Saunders and J. Fiske; and *A Dictionary of Communication and Media Studies* by J. Watson and A. Hill.

Agenda setting refers to the process by which the news media define which topics (the agenda) should be of main interest to the audience. Hence the media have a significant influence on issues for public discussion.

Audience   Those persons who are the receivers of a message, particularly of a mass media message. (Also called **receiver** or **destination**.)

Barriers to communication   Factors in the communication process that impede open communication between source and destination. (Also called **filters** or **noise**.) They exist within individuals (psychological filters), within the sign/message (semantic filters) and within the context (mechanical filters).

Channel   The means of communication through which messages flow from source to destination. Most examples of the communication process include multiple channels.

Code   A system of signs bound by conventions. The English language is a primary code (see also the notion of secondary codes).

Encoding refers to the process of translating ideas, feelings, opinions into signs following the conventions of a code (e.g. speaking or writing).

Decoding refers to the understanding and interpreting of signs (e.g. listening or reading).

Communication The process of creating and sharing meaning through the transmission and exchange of signs. This process requires interaction within oneself, between people, or between people and machines.

Consensus refers to the centre ground of beliefs and values agreed within a society. These are broadly held and proposed by the mass media. As expressed by the media consensus tends to exclude the notion of alternative or multiple views of a given topic or issue.

Context is the environment or surroundings in which communication takes place. Contexts may be physical or social/cultural.

Conventions are rules defining how signs are used within codes and how these signs, collectively, may be understood.

Culture A collection of beliefs, values and behaviours distinctive to a large group of people and expressed through various forms of communication. It is common to identify culture in terms of nation (e.g. French), or area (e.g. European), or race and religion (e.g. Jewish). Culture is represented through dress, religion and art forms in particular, as well as through language.

Popular culture generally refers to popular and commercial forms of art and media entertainment.

High culture generally refers to the culture of an educated and dominant class.

Folk culture generally refers to the culture which is created by people for themselves. It usually relies on oral traditions.

Mass culture generally refers to the popular culture shared by a mass media/consumer audience.

Feedback is communication in response to a previous message. It includes the idea that the sender adjusts his or her communication style in response to feedback. Feedback is continuous in conversation. It may be a deliberate response (e.g. a spoken reply) or an unintentional response (e.g. some non-verbal behaviours).

Gatekeeper refers to an individual within an organization who has some power to control and direct the flow of information into and out of that organization. This power may include the right to select information or even to interpret it (e.g. a news sub-editor).

Genre A term describing a recognizable body of work with common characteristics (e.g. science fiction). Genres are thus usually recognized within popular narrative fiction and art forms.

Image A picture, as seen in a photograph or single frame of film.
In literary criticism an image is an extended metaphor.

More broadly, image can refer to a mental conception of a person, place or thing (e.g. a brand image of a particular consumer product).

Information refers in the first place to factual communication, including verifiable and objective facts about the world.

More broadly the term can include anything which adds to our sum of knowledge about the world and people. In this case, beliefs and opinions given and received could be described as information.

Information serves to reduce uncertainty – you know more than you did before gaining the information.

Language is a widely used term referring to a system/code for organizing signs according to conventions. Learning how to use our native language is fundamental to becoming a social being. We use language for personal purposes (to think, organize our ideas and perceptions, and to imagine), for social purposes (to exchange messages with one another) and for cultural purposes (to record the past and to transmit ideas and values to the future).

Meaning   What is signified by a message conveyed through the signs that we give or receive. The meanings of messages are in our heads, not in their words or pictures. What a sender means by the signs offered may be different from what the receiver understands by the signs received. Levels of meaning are often distinguished in signs, for example, a sign serves to **denote** a generally agreed basic meaning within a culture and it also serves to **connote** broader personal and cultural associations (e.g. words like *slim, slender, thin, lean, skinny* have similar basic denotations but also suggest different connotations).

Medium/media   A channel or means of communicating. A medium usually comprises more than one form of communication. The word **media** has now come to refer to mass media. **Mediation** refers to the process of selection and interpretation which transforms material passing through the media.

Message   A unit of information, whether of fact or of opinion, passed via a channel. In most examples of the communication process more than one message is passed. It is the **content** of a piece of communication.

Overt messages are those which are apparent and obvious.

Covert messages are those which are concealed, intentionally or otherwise. They may well be messages about beliefs, opinions and attitudes.

NVC   Acronym for **non-verbal communication**. That is, the means of communication which includes body language, paralanguage and dress.

Perception refers to the process by which we make sense of the world and other people. It involves selecting, organizing and interpreting what we receive through our senses to create our own mental reality. Perception is a fundamental aspect of decoding meanings and depends on our knowledge, beliefs and experience.

Process refers to the act of communication, including the various factors which contribute to communication. Examples may be taken within any one of the four categories of communication (i.e. intrapersonal, interpersonal, group, mass). Communication is described as a process because it is not static.

Role   A part played by an individual within a given group and situation. This part includes selected personality traits and kinds of behaviour which help define that person's relationship with other people in a group (e.g. work roles or family roles).

Semiology   The discipline or area of study that examines signs and their meanings.

Sign   A single unit of communication which conveys a meaning (or meanings) that is learnt through education or socialization.

Most examples of communication include a flow of signs, perhaps through more than one channel, all of which interact. Anything which we can say has a meaning may be defined as a sign, whether it be a word or an object.

Socialization   The process through which we learn the dominant beliefs, values and behaviour acceptable within our society. So it is also concerned with learning to communicate. The family, work, school and the media are significant agents of socialization.

Stereotype   A simplified depiction of a person or group, in writing or in a picture, usually represented in the media. The type has a few dominant characteristics that make it easily identified (e.g. the nutty professor).

Strategy   A piece of communication with a purpose. The term usually refers to interpersonal communication in which we use strategies, learnt through experience, to achieve a purpose such as the breaking off of conversation.

Sub-culture   A cultural group within a dominant larger culture. The sub-culture nevertheless has its own distinctive characteristics and behaviour and beliefs (e.g. West Indian communities in Britain, Hell's Angels).

Transaction   A communication exchange, usually with functional connotations (e.g. withdrawing money from a bank). Two or more people agree to deal with one another (interact) to develop a relationship that will enable the exchange of meanings.

RESOURCES LIST FOR COMMUNICATION STUDIES

This selected resources list is arranged in three sections: books, other resources and addresses.

BOOKS

General communication, including theory and language

Berlo, D. K., *The Process of Communication*, New York, Holt Rhinehart & Winston, 1960 – readable account of linear models of communication. Simplistic behavioural perspective in places.

Britton, James, *Language and Learning*, Harmondsworth, Pelican, 1970 – explores the nature of language, its place in learning and thinking processes and the development of speech in children.

Cherry, Colin, *World Communication: threat or promise?*, revised edn, Chichester, Wiley, 1978 – world view of current and past developments in communication.

Corner, John, and Hawthorn, Jeremy (eds), *Communication Studies: an introductory reader*, London, Arnold, 1980 – collection of articles and extracts on five main aspects of communication studies. Intended for students on degree courses. Introductions to each section provide useful summaries.

Fiske, J., *Introduction to Communication Studies*, London, Methuen, 1982 – useful coverage of the communication process. Strong on linguistic approach. Has a great deal to say about semiotic approaches.

Hayakawa, S. I., *Language in Thought and Action*, New York, Harcourt

Brace Jovanovich, 4th edn, 1978 – thorough, linguistically informed and well-exemplified text on the ways in which we use language to think and to communicate for various purposes. Suggestions for activities.

McKeown, Neil, *Case Studies and Projects in Communication*, London, Methuen, 1982 – strong on working approach to case studies and projects; also an introduction to concepts. Discusses method from experience and examples.

McQuail, Denis, *Communication*, London, Longman, 1975 – comprehensive account of the traditions of mass media study: theory, functions, audience, institutions, effects.

McQuail, Denis, and Windahl, Sven, *Communication Models for the Study of Mass Communications*, London, Longman, 1981 – discusses purposes of 'modelling' and reproduces many different mass communication models.

O'Sullivan, Tim, Hartley, J., Saunders, D., and Fiske, J., *Key Concepts in Communication*, London, Methuen, 1983 – reference book with definitions and descriptions of terms used in communication studies.

Schramm, W., *Men, Women, Messages and Media*, New York, Harper Row, 2nd edn, 1982 – very readable account of the communication process and factors affecting it. Plenty of examples and models. The first half is most useful, dealing with the subject in general and with interpersonal communication. The second half is useful on principles and models, but, being about mass media, takes American examples.

Spender, Dale, *Man-made Language*, London, Routledge & Kegan Paul, 1980 – about the sexist bias of the English language illustrated with lots of examples.

Watson, James, and Hill, Anne, *Dictionary of Communication and Media Studies*, London, Edward Arnold, 1984 – contains entries on a large number of words and phrases. Useful source of reference.

Interpersonal and group communication

Argyle, Michael, *The Psychology of Interpersonal Behaviour*, Harmondsworth, Penguin, 3rd edn, 1978.

Argyle, Michael, *Social Interaction*, London, Methuen, 1969.
Argyle's books deal clearly with aspects of non-verbal communication and the processes of personal and group interactions.

Argyle, Michael, and Trower, Peter, *Person to Person*, London, Harper & Row, 1979 – compact and readable account of factors affecting interpersonal communication. Brightly illustrated, well related to everyday experience and clearly explained.

Berne, Eric, *What do you say after you say hello?*, London, Corgi, 1975 – transactional analysis (TA) approach to social interaction.

Gahagan, Judy, *Interpersonal and Group Behaviour*, London, Methuen, 1978 – small, inexpensive and gives basics.

Goffman, Erving, *The Presentation of Self in Everyday Life*, Harmondsworth, Pelican, 1959 – classic study of personal interaction in social institutions.

Morris, Desmond, *Manwatching*, St Albans, Triad Panther, 1978 – popular, brightly illustrated approach to non-verbal communication, including some cross-cultural perspectives. In an abridged edition too.

Myers, G. E., and Myers, M. T., *Dynamics of Human Communication*, New York, McGraw-Hill, 3rd edn, 1980 – American textbook for courses in speech communication, but it also deals with important areas of self-concept, non-verbal communication, perception, language and inter-personal skills. Readable, clearly laid out, with ideas for practical work.

Patton, B., and Giffin, K., *Interpersonal Communication in Action*, New York, Harper Row, 2nd edn, 1977 – readable account of processes and concepts of interpersonal communication. Summaries of other authors and helpful diagrams/models.

Sprott, W. J. H., *Human Groups*, Harmondsworth, Penguin, 1958 – simple, short and pretty clear.

Communication in business and organizations

Biddle, Derek, and Evenden, Robin, *Human Aspects of Management*, London, Institute of Personnel Management, 1980 – general account of human relationships in organizations written for 'managers'. Includes suggestions for activities.

Evans, Desmond W., *People and Communication*, London, Pitman, 1980 – summary of communication structures and conventions in 'business communication'.

Mitchell, T. R., *People in Organisations*, New York, McGraw-Hill, 1978 – thorough and pretty interesting in some examples given. Covers a lot of ground. Clearly structured. Definitely about the human factor/socio-psychology of institutions.

Myers, M. T., and Myers, G. E., *Managing by Communication: an organisational approach*, New York, McGraw-Hill, 1982 – written for students of business and management in the USA, it contains communication theory and practical work. Lots of case studies, assignments and simulations.

Pearce, John, *et al.*, *People in Touch*, London, Arnold, 1978 – useful collection of 'in role' case studies in 'business' contexts.

Stanton, Nicki, *What Do You Mean 'Communication'?: an introduction to communication in business*, London, Pan, 1982 – readable account of the processes and forms of communication in business. It includes useful exercises and case study materials.

Mass Media

Adams, C., and Laurikietis, R., *The Gender Trap 3: Messages and Images*, London, Virago, 1980 – simple and amusing account of gender stereotyping.

Alvarado, M., and Buscombe, E., *Hazell, The making of a TV series*, London, BFI/Latimer, 1978 – description and comment on the production of a popular thriller series.

Berger, John, *Ways of Seeing*, Harmondsworth, Pelican, 1972 – this and the BBC programmes (for hire) are still provocative essays on perception and the visual arts. In particular Berger presents original and well-argued ideas about how we have learnt to see advertising images and images of women.

Bilbow, M., *The Facts about a Feature Film*, London, André Deutsch, 1978 – simple description of the production of a horror film.

British Film Institute Television Monographs – booklets on television, note especially *Nationwide, Television News, Structures of Television, Broadcasting and Accountability*.

Cohen, Stanley, and Young, Jack, *The Manufacture of News: deviance, social problems and the mass media*, London, Constable, 2nd edn, 1981 – useful collection of articles and extracts. Summaries at various points also provide quick surveys of the themes.

Curran, J., and Seaton, J., *Power without Responsibility: the press and broadcasting in Britain*, London, Methuen, 2nd edn, 1985 – useful comprehensive coverage of the development of the press, radio and television. It takes a critical view of ownership, control and the encouragement of consensus views.

Dyer, Gillian, *Advertising as Communication*, London, Methuen, 1982 – study of advertising as a form of communication including cultural and semiological approaches.

Glasgow University Media Group, *Bad News*, London, Routledge & Kegan Paul, 1976 – 'Bad News', 'More Bad News', 'Really Bad News' – all carefully documented studies of TV news. Broadcasters contest the conclusions.

Hartley, John, *Understanding News*, London, Methuen, 1982 – comprehensive study of news collection, news values and news presentation as communication.

Hood, Stuart, *On Television*, London, Pluto Press, 2nd edn, 1983 – informed and pithy critique of television's institutions, practices and product. Useful introduction to terms and concepts in mass media studies.

MacShane, Denis, *Using the Media: how to deal with the press, television and radio*, London, Pluto Press, 1979 – direct and informative. The earlier sections especially present a lot of facts about, for example, who controls which media. The later sections are aimed at practising trade unionists and inform about media conventions and working practice.

Masterman, Len, *Teaching about Television*, London, MacMillan, 1980 – source of philosophy and practice for all teachers of television studies.

Monaco, J., *How to Read a Film*, Oxford, Oxford University Press, 1977 – useful introduction to getting the most out of watching films.

Morley, David, and Whitaker, Brian (eds), *The Press, Radio and TV: an introduction to the Media*, London, Comedia, 1983 – a brief readable summary of many of the central issues: history, structures, programming, new technology.

Murphy, Brian, *The World Wired Up: unscrambling the new communications puzzle*, London, Comedia, 1983 – useful summary and international perspective on new communication technologies.

Tracey, M., *Production of Political Television*, London, Routledge & Kegan Paul, 1977 – detailed study from in-house experience that really takes to pieces institutions, product, conventions, economics, power.

Tunstall, Jeremy, *The Media in Britain*, London, Constable, 1983 – contains a good deal of background factual material about British media since 1945.

Whitaker, Brian, *News Ltd: why you can't read all about it*, London, Comedia 1981 – one of a series of books published by Comedia. All are worth reading and critical of what the media offer.

Practical communication

Evans, Harold, *Editing and Design*, London, Heinemann, 5 vols, 1972–8, especially *Newsman's English* (1972) and *Pictures on a Page* (1978) – readable, entertaining, well-illustrated books by an experienced journalist.

Ferguson, Robert, *Group Film Making*, London, Studio Vista, 1977 – simple, concise and common-sense approach to film-making skills.

Lewis, Roger, and Inglis, John, *Report Writing*, Cambridge, National Extension College, 1982 – a self-study text with lots of advice and exercises on how to write reports.

Lorac, Carol, and Weiss, Michael, *Communication and Social Skills*, Exeter, Wheaton, 1981 – an account of practical video work in schools to encourage communication and social skills.

MacInnes, J., *Video in Education and Training*, London, Focal Press, 1981 – helpful advice for making videos. Focal Press also publish other practical manuals on media production.

Mitchell, John, *How to Write Reports*, London, Fontana, 1977 – clear guide to preparing and compiling formal reports.

Owen, D., and Dunston, M., *The Complete Video Handbook*, Harmondsworth, Penguin, 1982 – advice on video equipment and production.

Wright, Christopher, *Puffin Book of Photography*, London, Puffin, 1981 – straightforward account of practical photography at a basic level.

OTHER RESOURCES

Audio-visual materials

Addresses where these materials can be obtained are in the address list.

Barker, Peter, and Clarke, Mike, *Talking Pictures: an introduction to media studies* – filmstrip collection plus cassette commentary and printed teacher's notes. Section 1 deals with reading of images; section 2 deals with 'genres' in film and television; section 3 investigates the presentation of news. From Mary Glasgow Publications Ltd.

Reading Pictures and *Selling Pictures* – photo sheets, teacher's book, slides. Intended for 14–15-year-olds to introduce the analysis of meaning in photographic images as 'representations of reality'. From the British Film Institute (BFI) Education Department.

The BFI also produces many other slide collections and documentation for film analysis. Also available are film and video extracts (e.g. *Boys from the Blackstuff, Coronation Street*).

Choosing the News, Teachers' Protest, The Market, The Station, The Visit – simulations and exercises using photographs and printed material. From Society for Education in Film and Television (SEFT).

Simulations

Interplay – a collection of case studies, articles and simulations for group work. Other collections are available on *Communication* and *Psychology*. From Longman Group Ltd, Resources Unit.

Radio Covingham, Front Page, The Dolphin Project and *Airport Controversy* – are role-play simulations in a series of games available from European Schoolbooks Ltd.

Booklets

Engineering Your Communications – a booklet about communication skills needed by various levels of employees in engineering companies. Lots of examples and illustrations. Published by the Engineering Careers Information Service.

Vernon, Tom, *Gobbledegook*, London, National Consumer Council, 1980 – a critical review of official forms and leaflets, and how to improve them.

The Manager's Responsibility for Communication, Selection Interviewing, Industrial Relations – booklets published by the Industrial Society. These contain brief summaries and advice for people in industry.

Cutts, Martin, and Maher, Chrissie, *Writing Plain English*, 1980, published by the Plain English Campaign.

Magazines and journals

For communication studies all newspapers and magazines can provide a source of materials for linguistic and image analysis, but this section contains a brief list of magazines that contain frequent articles on aspects of communication.

Broadcast	(weekly)
Camerawork	(quarterly)
Campaign	(weekly)
City Limits	(weekly)
Independent Broadcasting	(quarterly)
Liberal Education	(quarterly)
Listener	(weekly)
Marketing	(monthly)
Media, Culture and Society	(quarterly)
Media Reporter	(quarterly)
New Internationalist	(quarterly)
New Society	(weekly)
New Statesman	(weekly)
Private Eye	(weekly)
Screen and Screen Education	(quarterly)
Spare Rib	(monthly)
Time Out	(weekly)
Spectator	(weekly)
UK Press Gazette	(weekly)
Women's Media Action	(bi-monthly)

Addresses and other information for these journals can be found in the current edition of *Willings Press Guide*.

ADDRESSES

The following organizations provide materials of interest to the student of communication such as free leaflets, handbooks, reports, publicity brochures, film hire, educational packages and courses.

Advertising Association, Abford House, 15 Wilton Road, London, SW1V 1NJ.

Advertising Standards Authority Limited, 15/17 Ridgmount Street, London, WC1E 7AW.

Audio-visual Productions, Hocker Hill House, Chepstow, Gwent, NP6 5ER.

BBC, Broadcasting House, Portland Place, London, W1.

British Film Institute, Education Department, 81 Dean Street, London, W1A 6AA.

Campaign for Press & Broadcasting Freedom, 9 Poland Street, London, W1.

Central Film Library, Chalfont Grove, Gerrards Cross, Bucks, SL9 8TN.

Centre for Contemporary Cultural Studies, University of Birmingham, PO Box 363, Birmingham 15.

Engineering Careers Information Service, Engineering Industry Training Board, Clarendon Road, Watford.

European Schoolbooks Limited, Croft Street, Cheltenham, Gloucestershire, GL53 0HX.

Guild Organisation Limited, Guild House, Oundle Road, Peterborough, PE2 9PZ (library of BBC, ITV and Open University films for sale and hire).

Independent Broadcasting Authority, 70 Brompton Road, London, SW3 1EY.

Industrial Society, PO Box 1BQ, Robert Hyde House, 48 Bryanston Square, London, W1H 1BQ.

Institute of Practitioners in Advertising, 44 Belgrave Square, London, SW1X 8QS.

Local Radio Workshop, 12 Praed Mews, London, W1.

Longman Group Limited, Resources Unit, 9/11 The Shambles, York.

Mary Glasgow Publications Limited, Brookhampton Lane, Kineton, Warwick, CV35 0BR.

Plain English Campaign, 131 College Road, Manchester, M16 0AA.

Rank Aldis, PO Box 70, Great West Road, Brentford, Middlesex, TW8 9HR.

Society for Education in Film and Television, 29 Old Compton Street, London, W1V 5PL.

Video Arts Limited, Dumbarton House, 68 Oxford Street, London, W1N 9LA.

Women's Media Action Group, c/o A Woman's Place, Hungerford House, Victoria Embankment, London, WC2.

INDEX